'THE BEAST'
# DIEGO COSTA

G'

Chris Davies graduated from the University of Brighton in 2007 with a degree in sport journalism. His passions in life include football, rugby union, travel, sports reading and writing, and spending time with his daughter, family and friends. *Diego Costa: 'The Beast'* is his second solo project following the publication of *Deadly Dimitar: The Biography of Dimitar Berbatov* (John Blake Publishing, 2009). He lives on Jersey, in the Channel Islands.

# CONTENTS

# CHAPTER 1

# BLUE IS
# THE COLOUR

'People always used to say that my game would fit the Premier
League perfectly and so the opportunity to sign for an
extremely famous club like Chelsea made me super-excited.'
Diego Costa, *Champions League Magazine*

When referee Lee Mason blew his whistle for the final
time to signal a 1–0 victory for Crystal Palace over
Chelsea in March 2014, it heralded renewed hope for Tony
Pulis' men in their fight against relegation, but for Chelsea
Football Club, the end of their challenge for the Premier
League title.

Although the defeat, at the tail end of the 2013–14
campaign, didn't mathematically rule José Mourinho's team
out of the title race, it left them relying completely on other
results, results which would not ultimately go their way. And
following the team's abject performance at Selhurst Park,
Mourinho made a thinly veiled attack on his team's forwards
for their continued profligacy in front of goal:

# DIEGO COSTA: 'THE BEAST'

[Branislav] Ivanović, [César] Azpilicueta, [Gary] Cahill, [John] Terry – they perform in the sun, on small pitches, on big pitches, against aggressive teams, not aggressive teams, possession teams and not possession teams. They perform every game from one day to last day. But you have other players who are fantastic in some games and they disappear in others.

Mourinho was understandably frustrated. The defeat against Palace coupled with an earlier loss on the road at Aston Villa and a third damaging result against Sunderland on 19 April had cost the club the chance of winning the title in his first season back in charge of the Blues. And it was as clear as day for all to see why. The manager knew it. The club's fans knew it. Television pundits and journalists never tired of mentioning it. But perhaps more significantly, the men under the spotlight knew it. Chelsea Football Club had almost certainly thrown away a golden opportunity to steal the 2013–14 Barclays Premier League title from under the noses of eventual champions Manchester City and the club of so many of the neutrals, Liverpool. There was an obvious reason for their capitulation and everybody could see it.

Their forward line consisting of £50 million man Fernando Torres, Samuel Eto'o and Demba Ba had between them contributed just nineteen league goals for the season. Meanwhile, Manchester City trio Edin Džeko, Sergio Agüero and Yaya Touré combined to score fifty-three, while Luis Suárez and former Chelsea forward Daniel Sturridge between them scored an astounding fifty-two for second-place Liverpool. Chelsea's main problem and reason for ultimate failure was obvious to everyone. Their forwards didn't contribute enough to the cause.

Following the disappointment in south London and ahead of the club's Champions League quarter-final tie with French champions Paris Saint-Germain, Mourinho reiterated his belief that certain players had cost his team dearly throughout the campaign:

> Clearly, during the season, we have players up and down in relation to the profile of the match. Stamford Bridge is better than away. Playing away against Arsenal or City or United or Liverpool is one thing, and another thing is to play Crystal Palace away or West Bromwich away or Stoke City away.

Nine years earlier, in his first season in west London and with the club celebrating their centenary season, the Portuguese had led Chelsea to their first championship success since their only other title win fifty years before. And after an ultimately disappointing campaign in 2014, which saw them finish third in the table and devoid of any silverware, Mourinho knew what he had to do. In the summer of 2014, empowered by Roman Abramovich's millions, he would do whatever was necessary to put Chelsea back on top. Waving goodbye to Stamford Bridge would be the club's record goalscorer Frank Lampard, long-serving left back Ashley Cole and David Luiz who joined Paris Saint-Germain for £50 million. With Torres' departure on the last day of the transfer window, a clean sweep of the club's strikers was completed when he followed Eto'o, Ba and Romelu Lukaku out of the exit door.

3

Fresh blood was required and established quality was the order of the day. Chelsea's squad already boasted a spine of top quality players including John Terry, Nemanja Matić and Eden Hazard. But they were short in vital areas and Mourinho set about resolving the team's deficiencies as soon as the transfer window reopened at the start of the summer. And his first major signing would be a player who had just inspired his Spanish employers to win their first league championship triumph in eighteen years. Brazilian-born Diego Costa was that man; his £32 million release clause the fee. And he was a player Mourinho knew well.

The Spanish international striker had joined Atlético Madrid in Spain's Primera División back at the tail end of 2006 when he was a raw eighteen-year-old. Following nomadic spells on loan at various clubs around Spain's lower reaches, the arrival of Diego '*El Cholo*' Simeone as Atlético's new head coach in December 2011 finally sparked Costa's professional career into life. He had suffered a serious knee ligament injury during pre-season training ahead of the 2011–12 La Liga campaign, but after spending the second half of the season out on loan regaining his fitness at Rayo Vallecano, he returned to the Vicente Calderón stadium ready to make his mark.

Following initial first-team rejection from Simeone, he proceeded to help Atlético break their fifteen-year winless hoodoo against city rivals Real Madrid, managed at the time by Mourinho, whilst winning Copa del Rey and La Liga titles in successive seasons. Costa had become a key player for Atlético in those two seasons on the red and white side of the Madrid divide, scoring fifty-six goals in all competitions. His spirit and sheer will to win was shared by Simeone and mirrored his own philosophy on football. He was a winner, willing to do the unglamorous jobs on the pitch in addition to banging home goal after goal. He was the team's first defender.

Simeone loved him and christened Costa 'El Cholo', after himself – 'the beast'. And Costa is in illustrious company. It is a nickname that has been adopted by many physical sporting stars in recent times. The Jamaican sprinter Yohan Blake, Tendai Mtawarira, the South African rugby union international, and Manu Vatuvei, the 250lb New Zealand rugby league winger all bear the same imposing nickname.

Having learnt his trade playing street football in his hometown like fellow South Americans Diego Maradona, Lionel Messi and Luis Suárez before him, Costa is an old-school footballer born perhaps in the wrong era. In today's football world, it is almost impossible to breathe on somebody without incurring the wrath of the crowd, the referee and the media. And Costa has become another victim of the success of modern-day football where every movement on the pitch is scrutinised to the maximum.

Back in the sixties, seventies and eighties, things were different. Football was different and more physical. In some ways it was a more innocent time where diving and feigning injury rarely happened as it does so often in today's game. Every team had their hard men ready to mix things up when necessary. There was Ron 'Chopper' Harris at Chelsea; Don Revie's Leeds United had Billy Bremner and Norman 'Bites Yer Legs' Hunter, while Liverpool, the dominant team of the seventies and eighties, boasted Graeme Souness and Tommy 'The Anfield Iron' Smith in their ranks. Football was full of hard men, willing to do whatever it took to win. Decades later, Costa nevertheless came from that very same school of thought. He hates to lose and Spain-based La Liga expert Sid Lowe conjured up a fantastic scene of domestic non-bliss concerning Costa's passion for winning in an article for the *Guardian* newspaper:

> Diego Costa says he never takes his work home with him. Which is probably a good thing. If he did, he might walk through the door, goad the dog with a stick, surreptitiously elbow his wife out of the way on the stairs, shrug his shoulders innocently as she lay in a crumpled heap at the bottom, and whisper insults to his children, look the other way and whistle when they burst into tears.

Football fans care more about their individual clubs than anybody else, including the owners, managers and players. They want to see people running, managing and playing for their team who care, or at least show that they care as much as they do. Some do. Many don't. For many involved in the game, money is the overriding motivation behind their desire to play football. There are still some in the game whose loyalty to their employer and to living out the dreams of the fans matter more than the riches on offer. And while the era of the 'one club for life' players appears to be almost over, there are those out there like Costa who give those on the terraces hope that they genuinely do care about what happens on the pitch.

Of course, in addition to managing Real Madrid against Costa's Atlético and watching the big man score a superb equaliser in the 2013 Copa del Rey final between the two city rivals, Mourinho had also watched Costa give Chelsea's central defensive partnership of John Terry and Gary Cahill first-hand experience of his physical attributes and uncompromising style in the semi-final of the Champions League in 2014. He also dispatched a nerveless and decisive penalty in the second leg at the Bridge to put Atlético on their way to the final. Mourinho, with his team out of league contention and now out of the Champions League, knew he had found the perfect man to lead his team from the front. Arriving on the back of a disappointing World Cup with Spain (Costa had been granted Spanish citizenship in September 2013), where the hosts crashed out at the first phase and the Brazilian public jeered his every move, Costa, who was nominated in a twenty-three-man shortlist for the 2014 FIFA Ballon d'Or award, was delighted to touch down in the English capital ready for the new challenge that lay ahead.

I am very happy to sign for Chelsea. Everybody knows it is a big club in a very competitive league, and I am very excited to get started in England with a fantastic coach and team-mates. Having played against Chelsea last season I know the high quality of the squad I am joining. I would like to thank everybody at Atlético who made me into the player I am; it was an incredible time for me, but now I am starting a new adventure and I hope to win many trophies with Chelsea.

After securing his main target for the summer in the opening days of the 2014 summer transfer window, Mourinho revealed in his press conference ahead of Chelsea's opening league match with Burnley that he had actually missed the opportunity to sign Costa way back in 2006–7 when he was playing at Sporting Braga: 'To be fair he was in Portugal [at Braga] at eighteen and I never looked at him. So everybody was blind including myself. He went to Atlético and [Sergio] Agüero was the superstar.'

In addition to bringing in their new number 19, Thibaut Courtois returned from a highly successful three-year loan spell at Atlético along with his team-mate Filipe Luís, while Mourinho also snapped up inspirational former Arsenal lynchpin Cesc Fàbregas, club legend Didier Drogba, and QPR and France forward Loïc Rémy in an attempt to bring the Premier League and Champions League crowns back to the King's Road.

In his first four games in the physically demanding English Premier League, Costa got off to a flying start, banging in seven goals including a hat-trick against Swansea City to surpass Sergio Agüero and Mick Quinn's record of six goals from their first four matches for Manchester City and Coventry City respectively.

Since arriving in England, Costa has continued to adopt the abrasive take-no-prisoners style of football that he grew up playing on the streets of his hometown, Lagarto. It is a style that has got him into trouble on several occasions in the past, but as the old adage says, if you take the devil out of a player, you ruin his game. The same was said about Wayne Rooney back in his early days and it can be said about Costa. That bite and aggression is what makes him so fascinating to watch. Indeed, never was this controversial style of play – controversial today, anyway – more evident than in the

League Cup semi-final clash between Chelsea and Liverpool at Stamford Bridge in late January 2015.

With the tie finely balanced from the first leg, stamping incidents involving Costa and Liverpool players Emre Can and Martin Škrtel overshadowed an absorbing contest which saw the home team prevail to advance to a first Wembley final since Mourinho's return to his spiritual home. *Sky Sports* pundit Gary Neville described the incidents in his newspaper column for the *Telegraph* as being 'a bit naughty'; that is exactly what Costa is, a bit naughty, but nothing more. Yes, he takes things to the limit. Yes, he sometimes crosses the line. But that is why he is so fascinating to watch and why he divides opinion in the football community.

Everybody it seems has an opinion on him. You either love him or hate him. Those who love him, or at the very least like or admire him – other than the supporters of the clubs he has quite literally given his heart and soul for – would probably include the older generation of football fan who were used to seeing tough men of the ilk of Harris, Hunter and Souness et al. Supporters of opposition clubs and the younger generation of fans who are now suffocated by how controversy-free the game should be, probably loathe him. However, if you were to conduct a survey and ask every football fan in the land if they would have Costa in their team given the chance, more likely than not the vast majority would take him in a heartbeat.

But Costa won't change. He's already admitted it. It's not in his make-up to change. He is what he is, take it or leave it. Mourinho and the Chelsea fans will most definitely take it, no questions asked. And speaking to the *Daily Telegraph* in late

January 2015, Costa rationalised how he sees football and how he sees his impact on the game:

I'm always loyal, I always go 100 per cent, I always go on the limit but I think the people that think that I am a violent player, it's because they interpret football a different way; they see it in a different way. Back in the old days there used to be way more contact and a lot of things that were permitted. These days everyone is looking at it and I don't think that is good for the game. I have a go at defenders and they have a go at me. We argue. Whatever happens on the pitch stays on the pitch. After the game I shake hands with the defender. Job done, I go home, he goes home. We're all mates. It's all good. That's how I see football. That's how I play football. I'm not going to change it – football is a contact sport.

And that is what most football fans love to hear, a player who actually likes a bit of contact in the game and is happy to give back what he has to take during a match. He may commit fouls, act 'a bit naughty' as Neville described it and cause controversy at times, but he is also one heck of a football player. Helping Chelsea to beat Tottenham Hotspur and pick up the first silverware of the season with the League Cup triumph at Wembley in March 2015, the chants of 'Diego, Diego' from the Blues supporters in the pouring rain would have been music to the ears of a player who strives to do his best every time he takes to the turf.

Twenty goals in just twenty-six Premier League appearances, one more than Torres, Eto'o and Ba could muster between them the previous campaign, and his all-action never-say-die attitude helped to inspire Jose's Chelsea to a fifth league title in the club's long and decorated history and also saw him taken to the hearts of the Blues faithful.

A second league title in successive seasons was the reward for Costa's hard work and goals. He is quite simply a winner. He's been hung, drawn and quartered so many times during his colourful career. However, if you were to ask him if he is bothered by the bad press he so often receives, his will to do the best he can for himself, the team and his family would probably mean that he couldn't care less. As he admitted in an interview with *Four Four Two*, his life off the pitch is completely in contrast to his life on it:

> I'm a different beast off the pitch. I'm relaxed and very happy. On it, I fight to continue to lead the life I have off it. Every time I score I'm happy for myself, of course, but I know it makes those I'm closest to more so, because they depend on me for their own lives.

# CHAPTER 2

# ADEUS BRASIL, OLÁ PORTUGAL

'I always had to be Ronaldo. I tried to copy everything he did.
Why? Because he was a beast, the best in the world.'
Costa reveals Brazil's legendary striker was his idol
while he was growing up in Lagarto, Sergipe

In the north-east of Brazil lies the state of Sergipe. It is the smallest of twenty-six states in the country and has the vast Atlantic Ocean to the east. The largest city in Sergipe is Aracaju, the state capital, and some 75 kilometres farther inland is the small and unremarkable town of Lagarto. The town is home to more than 100,000 people and the home town of Diego da Silva Costa. Lagarto is a municipality, one of 5,570 in the country, which means it has the constitutional power to approve its own laws and collect taxes while also receiving funds from the (Sergipe) state and the Brazilian federal governments. The economy of Sergipe is primarily supported by the production of sugarcane and oranges, yet the biggest export to come out of the state and Lagarto in particular is probably the footballer Diego Costa, Brazilian by birth, international striker for Spain at the time of writing and top goal scorer in the English Premier League for his club, Chelsea.

On 7 October 1988, Diego was born in Lagarto to proud parents José de Jesus and Josileide. By no stretch of the imagination is Lagarto an affluent area of South America's largest country. In fact his upbringing is about as far away from the lifestyle he now enjoys in west London as you can possibly get, an almost typical rags-to-riches story. Yet he is as proud of his roots as his hometown residents are of him, and he returns there whenever possible, as he told the *Telegraph* in an exclusive interview in March 2015: 'It's small and I'm very proud of my hometown. The weather is nice and I love going back there. Every time I have a holiday, I will go there. It's where my family still live, where they are based and I enjoy very much, going back there.'

Diego shares his birthday with Russian President Vladimir Putin, television producer and celebrity Simon Cowell and more relevantly, footballers Jermain Defoe and former Brazilian World Cup winners Gilberto Silva and Dida.

It is no secret that football is like a religion in South America. Some of the biggest stars ever to grace the sport have emerged from the Latin continent. Costa's father José has a genuine love for the game, and it is this love that shines through in both of his sons' forenames. Born just over two years after Napoli star Diego Armando Maradona almost single-handedly won the World Cup for Argentina in 1986, it was José who insisted that his second son should bear the name Diego.

Josileide had no choice in the matter. It was a bold statement from José because when it comes to football, Brazilians and

Argentinians don't just dislike one another, they loathe one another. There is no greater rivalry. Yet José was such a fan of football and so captivated by Maradona's genius on the pitch that the biggest tribute he could pay to his newborn son was to name him after the greatest player in the world at that time (some say ever). Yes there were great players in the Brazil setup at the time, players of the ilk of Sócrates, Careca, and not forgetting the ever-popular veteran Zico. All masters of the game, but none possessed the touch of a genius the way Maradona did.

Diego's older brother had also received the star name treatment. But the elder sibling's name came from a much less contentious source. In 1970, Brazil winger Jairzinho became the only footballer in history to score in every round of the World Cup finals, seven in total, including the final. As part of Mario Zagallo's dream team containing star attractions such as Pelé, Tostão, Rivelino, Gérson and Carlos Alberto Torres, Brazil wiped the floor with all before them, winning the final at a canter with a 4–1 demolition of Italy in Mexico City. Subsequently, Diego's brother was named Jair in honour of one of his country's greatest players. Knowingly or unknowingly, a theme had been set by José and Josileido. Both of their sons were now named after wonderful footballers who had both lifted the World Cup trophy in the hugely atmospheric Azteca Stadium in Mexico's capital city.

Indeed, naming one's children after famous footballers is normal practice within Brazil. It is a popular occurrence the world over in fact, but usually parents tend to restrict naming their child to just the forename, such as in the case of Dennis Bergkamp, who was named after former Manchester United and Scotland star Denis Law by his football-loving parents. In a special programme recorded for the BBC ahead of the 2014 World Cup, former England captain Gary Lineker discovered that José's decision to name his son after the greatest play of Brazil's eternal rivals, Argentina, is accepted as perfectly normal within the country. The programme also revealed a number of other more unusual names which have been logged with registrars around the country that employ the surname, or sometimes the first name and the surname, including Lineker Hoffmann, Rummenigge da Silva, Jorge Beckenbauer, Michel Platini Goes, Klinsmann Carrilho, Ruud Gullit Ribeiro and Diego Maradona da Silva.

Unsurprisingly, from an early age, football formed a pivotal part of the young Diego's life. His father did as most fathers do in Brazil – he bought his son a football. As Diego explained to the *Telegraph*: 'In Brazil, if you have a son, the first thing you give him is a football. That's the first gift – so my dad was no different.'

Like Maradona before him, Diego admits to having honed the aggressive physical skills and attributes that are so evident in his game today as a child, playing with his friends on the streets of Lagarto. He has developed into one of the world's most feared strikers. Renowned for his tenacity and never-say-die attitude on the pitch, he admitted how he had struggled to contain himself as a child to *Four Four Two* magazine in December 2014:

The street had been my school. I fought with everyone. I couldn't control myself. I insulted everyone, I had no respect for the opposition – I thought I had to kill them. Boys who grew in academies are taught to control themselves and respect others, but no one ever told me otherwise. I was used to seeing players elbowing each other in the face and thought it was the norm.

He was just like any other kid in Brazil, in South America in fact. Football was everything. It meant everything. Once school was over for the day, there was no sitting in front of the television or playing on computer consoles. His mother Josileide wasn't to allow slacking in school either. He was expected to behave and get good grades when in school. If he did as his mother demanded she would allow him to go and play his football. And if you wanted to find Diego after school, you'd find him with all the other boys and sometimes men playing football in the street, learning their trade. But not learning his trade in a conventional sense. There was no academy for gifted players in Lagarto. There was no professional scouting network trawling through the streets looking for the next Pelé, Maradona or Lionel Messi. Today there is an academy in Lagarto thanks to the generosity of Costa himself, who wanted to give something back to his hometown and local community to give youngsters an opportunity that he wasn't fortunate enough to benefit from himself.

In fact the town didn't even have its own club until 2009. And even now the standard is very low with Lagarto FC competing in the Sergipe state championship. There was and still is no professional club within 300 kilometres. Esporte Clube Vitória, based in the city of Salvador in the neighbouring state of Bahia, was probably the closest. To put it in context, the nearest professional club to his hometown was approximately the same distance as it is to travel from London to Leeds. But none of that mattered at the time to a young Diego. He just loved to play football, as his father José explained to *Four Four Two*:

> The first thing he would do [when he got home from school] would be to grab a ball and go out onto the street and play. He was obsessed. He moved so well and learned on the street how to use his body to his advantage. And he hated losing. If he ever lost at anything, he'd spend the rest of the day seriously pissed off. He's been a fighter since the day he was born. Winning is all that matters. He plays every game as if it's his last.

It is a trait that Costa has brought forward into his professional career. Put simply, he hates to lose. On occasions, his will to win gets the better of him. And he can cut a frustrated figure when things are not going according to plan for his team. Never was his passion to succeed more evident than in the crucial second leg of the Champions League match with Paris Saint-Germain at Stamford Bridge. Visibly incensed by a perceived lack of effort from his team-mates to close down and press the visitors, who despite being a man lighter after Zlatan Ibrahimović's sending off were still bossing the possession, he let out an angry roar of frustration. But that is just Diego. He wears his heart on his sleeve and isn't afraid to show his emotions on the pitch.

Growing up in the nineties there was no room for discussion when it came to having an idol. For Diego it had to be Ronaldo – '*el fenomeno*'. A World Cup winner, albeit as an unused squad member in 1994 as a seventeen-year-old, the buck-toothed striker from Rio de Janeiro would blossom into the world's greatest player and a hero to millions of aspiring Brazilians back home. He won the first of his two Ballon d'Or awards after scoring forty-seven goals in forty-nine games for Barcelona in 1996–97 at the age of just twenty-one under the guidance of the late Sir Bobby Robson, who at the time employed Mourinho as a translator and coach at the Catalan giants. A young Diego, like so many others, idolised Ronaldo. He told *Four Four Two*: 'My friends pretended to be others, but I always had to be Ronaldo. I tried to copy everything he did. Why? Because he was a beast, the best in the world. You couldn't take your eyes off him; it was like time stood still. He overcame massive obstacles and will always be a leader. A phenomenon.'

Diego loved living in Lagarto. He was surrounded by family and he had his older brother Jair who would always look out for him. But with no semblance of real prospects for the future, in 2004 and at the age of just fifteen he left the town in search of an opportunity to build a future for himself. He packed his bags and travelled the 2,000 kilometres to São Paulo, the largest city in South America and a sprawling urban metropolis. It was a tough decision for a teenager to have to make, but it was a chance Diego knew he had to take:

> My biggest challenge was leaving home in Lagarto. I left my parents in tears as I crossed the doorstep on my own. As you can imagine, it was hard. I was very bonded to the small village I am from. In my village, we all are very close to our families and it's unusual to end up living in

a different way to your relatives. However, I love them more than anything else. I always knew that I wanted to change my family's life.

In São Paulo he lived with and worked for his uncle Jarminho who ran a shop in the city. And it was actually Jarminho who would set Diego on his path to glory by introducing his young nephew to agents and scouts who occasionally passed by his shop. Diego was offered a trial at Barcelona Esportivo Capela, a small semi-professional club in São Paulo, not the world-famous Barcelona he would be facing within a matter of years.

This was his opportunity. If he could perform well in the trial, they might sign him on a paid contract. He had to give it his best shot. However, having had no formal training, he would have to put into practice what he had learned from playing against men and boys on the street. And that meant being tough on the pitch and showing no fear. And no fear is exactly what the young Diego demonstrated as the club's president Paulo Moura explained to *Four Four Two*:

We had this promising, strong defender called Felipe. Diego wasn't scared: he battled for every ball like it was a fight. They were almost punching each other. He arrived as a complete unknown and one week later was already in the team, scoring four goals in a game at an under-17 tournament. It's very unusual for a player in Brazilian football to come straight from the streets at that age [fifteen]. We knew he was something special.

Diego had achieved his first goal and a contract to play

football, every boy's dream. It wasn't the highest standard of football, but it was a start. He was getting paid around £100 a month, or just under 500 Brazilian Reais (the local currency) to play football. He possessed all the components to be a good player but he was still very raw. The professional clubs from the city, including Palmeiras, Portuguesa and São Paulo themselves, had all turned down invitations to come and take a look at him strutting his stuff on the pitch. And his inexperience on the field would count against him in a way that would almost take his life in a completely different direction. In a match for his club Barcelona, Costa, consumed by frustration on the field and unable to channel it correctly, punched an opponent, which led to him being suspended from playing football for four months. Disaster!

Not only was he unable to play for his club: he would miss out on the opportunity to play a match in front of a representative of Jorge Mendes, the super-agent who now boasts the likes of José Mourinho, Luiz Felipe Scolari, Cristiano Ronaldo, James Rodríguez, Ángel Di María, Radamel Falcao et al as clientele. Mendes, through his hugely successful agency Gestifute, founded in 1996 and now the biggest football agency in the world, would identify foreign talent and bring it to one of his company's partner clubs, which included Portuguese giants FC Porto, Sporting Braga, Benfica and Spanish giants Atlético Madrid. This should have been Diego's big opportunity to showcase himself to the world's most powerful football agent. But he was suspended. However, talking to Spanish newspaper *El Pais* some years later, Costa explained how, for reasons unknown to him, he was allowed to take part in the match. And he impressed those observing to such an extent that he was rewarded with a contract to play for S.C. Braga in the Portuguese SuperLiga: 'One day a man who worked for Jorge Mendes came to see me. I don't know why I was allowed to play that day. I don't know if it was him [Mendes] or God, but I played. When the game was over, this person offered me a contract to play for Sporting Braga, and that's how I came to Europe.'

His world had been turned upside down. This was it. He'd hit the big time, an opportunity to play football for a living and support his family in the process. It was everything he had dreamed of.

The state of Sergipe had never been renowned for producing sports stars. Indeed, only two of any real note had ever emerged from the tiny northern state, and none for over thirty years. The biggest and most successful star to come out of the state was the former Brazil midfielder Clodoaldo, who was born in the state capital Aracaju in 1949. A World Cup winner in 1970, he is most recognisable to football fans worldwide for his part in the build-up to Brazil's fourth goal in the final, finished emphatically by Carlos Alberto Torres after Pelé's perfectly timed assist. Earlier in the build-up to the goal, Clodoaldo had dribbled effortlessly past four Italian players, which prompted the immortal commentary from Kenneth Wolstenholme: '... and it's four, that was sheer delightful football.'

Clodoaldo played alongside Pelé and World Cup-winning captain Carlos Alberto Torres at Santos and went on to win the Campeonato Paulista or São Paulo state championship on five occasions and the Brazilian National Championship once, in 1968. The only other star of note to emerge out of Sergipe was João Batista Nunes, a striker who was born 97 kilometres north of Aracaju in the tiny municipality of Cedro de São João. Nunes' greatest triumphs as a footballer came during one of his five spells at the Flamengo football club based in Rio de Janeiro. He won the Brazilian National Championship twice, the 1981 Copa Libertadores and the 1981 Intercontinental Cup against Liverpool Football Club. The Intercontinental Cup, contested between the winners of the European Cup, as it was known at the time, and the Copa Libertadores champions, enabled Nunes to write his name into history as his two goals guided a Flamengo team featuring Zico to beat a stellar Liverpool side fielding internationals of the stature of Kenny Dalglish, Graeme Souness and Alan Hansen, 3–0.

Costa was now on his way to adding his own name to the shortlist of famous Sergipe exports. But there was the obvious drawback: he would have to become just that, an export, to do it. He would have to leave Brazil and his family. His father José wasn't overly keen on the idea. He didn't want his eighteen-year-old son to take the risk, especially as an offer had been put on the table for him to join Brazilian top-flight team São Caetano, located close by in the Greater São Paulo Metropolitan Area. However, despite having the opportunity to remain in Brazil and in a city that research suggests has the highest standard of living in the country, Diego opted to fly the nest and head to Portugal for the north-western district of Braga. His proper professional football career was about to begin. José revealed there was nothing that could be said to dissuade his passionate son from heading to Europe: 'We didn't want him to go. It seemed too much of a risk. He could've gone to São Caetano, a good option for him, but he said he'd given his word to Braga and he had to stand by it.

He was so bloody stubborn. "If you don't let me go, I'll just leave anyway.""

And so the time had come. He headed to Portugal alone. José even turned down the opportunity of a job working for the construction company owned by Braga's president. His parents were too embedded in Brazilian life to accompany their son halfway across the world. José and Josileide's life was in Lagarto. Diego would have to make the move to create a better life for himself and his family alone, his first move away from the comfort and support of his loved ones.

However, although he was heading for a foreign country, there was the added comfort that he would not have to adapt to learning a new language, the common language of Portugal and Brazil being Portuguese. The municipality of Braga also enjoys a Mediterranean climate, which meant the warm weather would enable Diego to settle more easily than if he had been snapped up by a club in one of Europe's colder stamping grounds for Brazilian youngsters, such as the Ukraine. And being home to approximately 180,000 inhabitants, his new home of Braga was tiny in comparison to São Paulo where the population tops 11 million, more than the whole of Portugal put together.

Sporting Braga had only recently partnered themselves with Diego's new agent Jorge Mendes. The partnership meant that Mendes' agency would scout and provide a number of players for the club with a view to enabling Braga to challenge the supremacy of the country's big three clubs – Porto, Benfica and Sporting Lisbon – and also to make themselves known on the European stage. And within five seasons that is exactly what they would go on to achieve together, with Braga breaking the stranglehold of the domestic big three to finish second in the league in 2009–10 for the first time in their history. The club also went on to play in the Champions League for the first time before reaching the final of the Europa League in 2011, losing 1–0 to Porto, before winning the Portuguese League Cup in 2013. Braga's president admitted his satisfaction at the rate of success enjoyed between his club and Mendes in the March 2015 edition of *Four Four Two* magazine: 'I always told Jorge that my ambition was for this club to be a champion club, and thanks to Jorge that's what happened.'

However, before eighteen-year-old Diego could make his debut for his new employers, he was shipped off 60 kilometres south to play on loan for F.C. Penafiel in the Portuguese second division, the club having being relegated from the Primeira Liga the previous season. Located to the east of Porto, Diego would be learning his trade playing under the tutelage of Rui Bento, the club's head coach and a member alongside Luís Figo and Rui Costa of Portugal's 1991 Under-20 World Cup-winning golden generation.

Speaking to regional Internet TV station valsousa.tv after moving to Penafiel to gain first-team experience, Diego said:

> Everybody is recognising my work. There's nothing better than progressing professionally. For me it was a good option to come here. I thank God everything is working well. I can't complain. The first two weeks were difficult. It's a different pace of life here, Braga is a bigger city, they live differently there. But everybody here helped me to adapt very quickly.

In thirteen matches for the Rubro-Negros, Diego helped himself to five league goals, a decent return for a rookie, before returning to Braga for the second half of the Primeira League campaign. Penafiel would go on to finish safely in mid-table with forty-one points, fourteen points clear of the relegation zone. Yet, in the five matches in which Diego found the back of the net, Penafiel didn't lose once and picked up eleven points from a possible fifteen, also beating eventual Liga de Honra champions Leixões 3–0 in his penultimate match for the club. Without him Bento's team would have been much closer to the danger zone. Bento saluted Costa's enthusiasm and ability in *Four Four Two* magazine in December 2014: 'You see those kinds of players at seventeen or eighteen and they have exceptional quality. That's what Diego was like. He wanted to be somebody in football.'

It would not be the last time in his career that Diego would be thankful to Bento for his guidance. Before his first year living in Portugal was out, Diego, still just eighteen, secured a move that would change his life for the second time in twelve months. Having impressed during his short stint with Penafiel, Bento recommended Diego to Atlético Madrid scout Javier Hernandez, who endorsed his judgement and Diego was signed to the Spanish giants. After the Spanish club paid the princely sum of €1.5 million for Diego's signature, Hernandez explained how Costa's arrival in Madrid had come about:

Rui told me he had this kid of seventeen who he liked a lot, so I called Atlético and they told me to stay one more day and check him out. They took me to Chaves, which is in the middle of nowhere, for this second division game.

The standard was horrible, like the third division in Spain. There were a load of old guys and this overgrown kid who was fighting everyone. He wasn't scared of anything – an incredible personality. Technically, he was brilliant; he just needed to understand his body better because he was slightly uncoordinated. But just look at him now. He's a beast.

After returning north to Braga, this time on-loan from his new employers Atlético Madrid, Costa would make his top-flight debut for the first team at the end of January against Paços de Ferreira from the substitutes' bench. With the team trailing by a single goal at half-time, head coach Rogério Gonçalves summoned Diego from the bench. His opportunity had arrived, and he would be replacing a legend of Portuguese football on the pitch, the team's star man João Pinto. Pinto had joined Braga at the start of the season following a career that had seen him spend time at all of Portugal's biggest teams bar FC Porto. Renowned for his ball skills and knack of scoring important goals, England football supporters will probably remember him best for his acrobatic headed goal against them at Euro 2000 when Portugal recovered from a two-goal deficit to win their group match 3–2 on their way to the semi-finals.

Yet, like Costa in the coming years, Pinto was also an aggressively committed player, regularly receiving his marching orders during a colourful career. And perhaps the lowest point of his career was at the 2002 World Cup in Asia, when, after being dismissed for a terrible tackle on Park Ji-sung of South Korea, Pinto struck the referee, leading to a subsequent six-month suspension from football and the end of his international career at the age of just thirty.

Costa played forty-five minutes against Paços but despite Braga recovering from a three-goal deficit to narrow the score to 3–2, his first match for his new club was destined to end in defeat. The very next game witnessed Costa line up for his first start for Os Arsenalistas at their home ground, the Estádio Municipal de Braga, also known as 'The Quarry', against CD Aves. And it would prove a winning full debut as Braga prevailed 1–0 thanks to a late goal from his fellow Brazilian forward Zé Carlos. Costa played the full ninety minutes again in a 1–0 away defeat at Leiria, Braga's sixth loss of the season already. But the defeat would prove the last in charge for Gonçalves who was fired immediately after the game's completion to be replaced the very next day by former Porto captain and ex-Portugual international Jorge Costa.

The new man's first match in charge of Braga saw the team head to the north of Italy to face Parma in the second leg of the UEFA Cup. Diego was back on the bench for the match, with Braga holding a slim 1–0 advantage from the first leg in Portugal a week earlier. But with Parma, twice winners of the UEFA Cup during the nineties, pressurising, the new coach threw Diego on in place of Zé Carlos with twenty minutes remaining. And despite the team being reduced to ten men with fifteen minutes remaining, Diego would reward his coach's show of faith in him with one minute of the match to go when he latched onto a right -wing cross to crash home a superb volley and put his team through to face Tottenham Hotspur in the last sixteen. For Diego it was a first goal in

Braga red. The joy and relief on his face and that of his team-mates was palpable.

Diego would go on to make just five further appearances for Braga before the end of the season including a cameo which saw him win a penalty in a 3–2 home defeat against Spurs in the Europa League. But, in what would turn out to be his final appearance for the Portuguese team who would finish the season in fourth position, Costa would show a side of his game that now divides public opinion on the type of player he has become. Facing Benfica and a team containing the likes of Rui Costa, Simão and David Luiz, Costa received a yellow card after coming on as a second-half substitute for his shocking high tackle on Benfica midfielder Petit's upper leg.

But for Diego, after missing Braga's final five matches of the season, a new challenge, a new language and a new home lay in wait across the Iberian Peninsula.

# CHAPTER 3

# THE LOAN SHARK

'The day you behave like a hard, aggressive worker and train at 100 per cent, you'll play in whatever team you desire.'
Costa's coach Maximo Hernandez attempts to motivate a young and naïve Diego while he is on loan at Albacete

**W**hen eighteen-year-old Diego Costa arrived back in Madrid on the back of loan spells with Portuguese teams FC Penafiel and Sporting Braga, any thoughts going through his mind that he would be able to force his way into Javier Aguirre's first-team picture were seriously wide of the mark. Despite the departure of the club's captain and darling of the Atleti supporters, Fernando 'El Nino' Torres, to English Premier League giants Liverpool, Atlético spent heavily in the summer of 2007 to bring in attacking reinforcements.

Diego Forlán, winner of the European Golden Boot award and the Pichichi award for the top goalscorer in Spain, arrived at the Vicente Calderón from La Liga rivals Villarreal in a multi-million pound deal. In addition, José Antonio Reyes signed on from Arsenal, Portuguese international Simão Sabrosa winged his way in from Benfica and Luis García arrived from Liverpool as part of the deal to take Torres to Anfield. The club also boasted the attacking prowess of the precociously gifted Sergio Agüero, son-in-law of Diego Maradona who had arrived at the age of eighteen in 2006 for a bumper €20 million from Argentine outfit Independiente. The competition was tough and uncompromising. Aguirre had replaced Torres with some top-drawer new men and although Costa was held in high regard by many at the Rojiblancos, his time to shine would have to wait. He was still just a raw teenager and having had no formal training as a youngster he needed time to find himself and learn his trade in the cutthroat business of professional football.

It all pointed to another loan spell. However, rather than sending him back over the border to Portugal, Aguirre and the club opted to keep him in Spain, which would allow them to monitor his progress more closely. His next destination would be Vigo in the north-west of Spain in what would be his third loan spell since arriving in Europe just over a year earlier. The city of Vigo is located in Galicia and is home to approximately 300,000 inhabitants. The city also boasts a multicultural and large proportion of South American and Portuguese expatriates, ensuring Costa, despite his tender years, would stand a good chance of settling in with so many Portuguese-speaking people already residing in the city.

Costa arrived at Os Celestes on the back of the club's relegation to Spain's Segunda División, Celta having finished the previous campaign in eighteenth position in La Liga. And in June 2007, the club, having been in existence since 1923, came dangerously close to liquidation due to a huge number of debts accrued. It was all a far cry from Celta's relative glory years of the late nineties when it established itself as a top-six club. The fans had grown used to having star players of the calibre of gifted Russian playmaker Aleksandr Mostovoi, his international team-mate Valeri Karpin and the French defensive midfielder Claude Makélélé, who would go on to represent Real Madrid, Chelsea and Paris Saint-Germain in a highly distinguished club and international career. For the time being at least, star names and major signings were confined to the history books.

The financial issues surrounding the club meant Costa was arriving at a club fighting not only for its future on the pitch but off it too. Having assumed control of the day-to-day running of the Galicians the previous April with the club heading for relegation, Costa's coach at Os Celestes would be none other than Bulgarian superstar Hristo Stoichkov. A key member of Johann Cruyff's all-conquering 'Dream Team' at Barcelona during the nineties and a Golden Boot winner at the 1994 World Cup finals in the United States where he inspired his country to a surprise fourth-place finish, Stoichkov had taken over a club in turmoil.

With the club financially stricken, a number of star players were ushered towards the exit as a period of austerity was invoked by the board to cut costs and meet creditor demands. It all meant that Stoichkov, formerly the manager of his country for three years before resigning following a bad patch, would have to rely on reserve team players, inexpensive purchases and loan deals for the campaign ahead. It was a difficult situation for everyone at the club, the manager included and not least for a young and inexperienced man such as Costa to arrive into. But for the rookie Brazilian striker this was the reality, and it was at least another opportunity to show off his undoubted potential. Stoichkov did manage to recruit some highly talented players to the club – Costa's future Atlético team-mate Mario Suárez included – and also his future Real Valladolid striking partner, Michu. Yet, a difficult season would ensue.

Celta got their campaign underway with a 1–1 draw at home to newly promoted Córdoba as they sought to somehow try and fight their way back up to the more lucrative top flight despite their obvious financial limitations. A 2–1 defeat followed at the hands of Castellón before Costa made his full debut for the club in a disappointing 1–0 home loss to another newly promoted team, Eibar. Indeed, it would take Costa four matches to get off the mark for his new team and it would prove an eventful evening for Stoichkov's new loan signing.

Facing Xerez at Celta's Balaídos stadium, Costa showed the two sides of his still naïve character when firstly he scored his maiden goal for his new employers, finishing from close range. Then, with the team having recovered from a goal deficit to go 3–1 ahead thanks to Costa's goal and a wonder strike from fellow new boy Suárez, the Brazilian teenager proceeded to earn himself a red card needlessly. After an unnecessary bout of show-boating late on, Costa got embroiled in an argument with a frustrated member of the Xerez team and found himself dismissed for the first time in his fledgling career.

After picking up just ten points from a possible twenty-one available with only three wins from seven matches, Stoichkov was sacked in early October despite the 3–1 victory over Xerez with the club sitting inadequately in the bottom half of the league table. Promotion was already beginning to look a tall order. The Bulgarian legend who had only been at the helm for six months and seventeen games departed Vigo having won just seven of his matches in charge and was replaced by Juan Ramón López Caro, a man who had managed the mighty Real Madrid for six months back in 2006 following the Galacticos' dismissal of ex-Brazil coach Vanderlei Luxemburgo.

López Caro arrived on the back of maintaining Levante's La Liga status in 2006–7, following the club's promotion back to the top flight the previous season. And his new task was to get Celta back up and challenging for promotion by the end of the season. With Costa available again after serving his one-match suspension, the new man in charge called him back into the team and following an eight-match unbeaten streak, which included six draws and just two wins, Celta welcomed Sevilla Atlético to the Balaídos and came away with a 2–1 victory, López Caro's third in charge of the club. However, it was to prove another learning chapter in the Costa manual when he received his marching orders for the second time that season with just twenty minutes played, leaving his team-mates to fight gallantly for the remaining seventy minutes to gain the three points despite their one-man disadvantage.

In his absence, Celta lost their next fixture 3–1 on the road to Cádiz, the team's first defeat under their new coach, before ending the year with a 4–1 victory over Granada 74 to give the home fans some Christmas cheer. It had been a frustrating first half-season in Vigo for Costa. He had accrued more red cards than goals and had only started seven of his twelve matches for the team, although that total would probably have increased to nine without the two enforced suspensions.

After the mid-season festive break, Celta returned to action with a 3–2 loss against Tenerife before winning two of their next three fixtures, Costa notching his second goal for the club in a 3–2 win over losing 2001 UEFA Cup finalists, Alavés. Two further defeats for the club followed as their hopes of an instant return to the Primera División began to look bleak, despite Costa getting on the score sheet for the second time in four matches in the defeat to Eibar.

One win, a draw and two defeats in the club's next four matches saw López Caro fall victim to the club's quick-fire approach to hiring and firing managers following a 1–0 loss on the road at Xerez. Replacing López Caro, with the club slipping dangerously towards the drop zone and a second successive demotion to Segunda División B for the first time since 1981, Celta promoted assistant coach Antonio López to the hot seat. And despite losing his first game in charge 1–0 at the hands of mid-table Albacete, it would be Costa who would inspire his new mentor to a first league victory in charge of Os Celestes with two goals on the road at Numancia as Celta came away victorious 2–1.

Entering the fray from the substitutes' bench at half-time with high-flying Numancia a goal to the good on home turf, Costa equalised for Celta before scoring one of the goals of the season with eleven minutes of the match remaining. Picking the ball up in his own half close to the centre circle, Costa turned and accelerated away with ease from the chasing midfielders before sprinting past the oncoming centre half and sliding the ball to the goalkeeper's left and into the net. It was a brilliant goal and an indication of the pace and power he possessed. He just needed somebody to harness the potential that Penafiel boss Rui Bento and Atlético scout Javier Hernandez had spotted in him.

After the impressive 2–1 win in north-western Spain against Numancia who would go on to be promoted to La Liga, Celta embarked on a run of form which saw them come to within just two points of being relegated for the second successive season. Costa again saw red in a 2–2 draw with Tenerife in the third last game of the season, his third dismissal of the campaign. For Celta, a difficult season did at least end with the club avoiding relegation. However, it would be a further two seasons before the club would eventually be able to celebrate promotion back to the top flight.

Meanwhile, Costa, despite showing glimpses of his undoubted potential with five goals during his season-long loan stay in north-west Spain, had also shown an immature side to his game with three red cards in thirty appearances. He would need to learn the lessons of his time in Vigo if he wanted to progress and build a career for himself in Madrid at some point in the future. Even so, his ability was evident even at such an early age, and Celta's goalkeeper Esteban, who could see his young team-mate's potential during his time in Vigo, was quoted as saying in *Four Four Two* magazine: 'He had real power and potential, similar to the original Ronaldo. But he was still very young, a player with great potential rather than a reality yet. It was hard for him; he came to a club that was not going back up, where there was tension and pressure. Players went unpaid.'

Following a historic summer that saw Spain being crowned

European Championship winners for the first time in the country's history, courtesy of former Atlético Madrid striker Fernando Torres' only goal in the final in Vienna against Germany, Costa was once again shipped out on loan for the forthcoming season, his fourth loan spell in total and third since being bought by Atleti.

This time, in his nomadic journey around Portugal and Spain, he landed up in the city of Albacete, just over 160 miles south-east of Madrid and a city of roughly 173,000 inhabitants. Based in the historic region of La Mancha to the south-east of the country, the city, despite being a commercial and industrial hub, also boasts large green areas and a reputation for being one of the ten cities with the lowest presence of pollution in the whole of Europe. Albacete Balompié were another Segunda División club, having last played in La Liga during the 2004–5 season, which had ended in relegation. The club, although not one of Spain's biggest, boasts a history of producing a number of players who would go on to star on bigger stages, including legendary former Real Madrid defender, José Antonio Camacho, ex-Spain striker Fernando Morientes and Barcelona's double European Championship and World Cup winner Andrés Iniesta. Indeed, in 2011, with Albacete struggling financially, Iniesta would become the club's major shareholder.

In Costa's first match for the city's team since arriving from Madrid, he introduced himself to the 5,000 fans in attendance at the club's 17,200 capacity Estadio Carlos Belmonte in the best way possible. Albacete had led 1–0 at the break before being pegged back five minutes from time by their opposition, Sevilla Atlético (also known as Sevilla B). However, with the final whistle approaching, Costa, wearing his now customary number 19 shirt, volleyed home from close range to give Albacete a 2–1 opening day victory to the delight of his new supporters.

The club followed up their opening day victory with an underwhelming run of results when they only managed one further win against Gimnàstic in their next seven fixtures, losing three in the process. An early goal from Costa, powering home a low right-footed shot from the edge of the area settled the team in their fixture against newly promoted Huesca. Costa missed further opportunities to extend the visitors' lead but when Albacete doubled their advantage before half-time through Basque-born midfielder Carlos Merino it looked as if a third win of the season was on the cards. However, following Merino's dismissal for a second yellow card before half-time, Huesca pulled a goal back and when Albacete were reduced to nine men late on the team were relieved to hold on for a much-needed win.

A 1–1 draw with Costa's former club Celta Vigo followed before the Brazilian youngster once again displayed the good and bad in his game in a 2–1 victory over Alicante on the Costa Blanca. With the teams having exchanged early goals, Albacete's having come from a delightful free kick, Costa, in the thirtieth minute, picked up the ball just inside the hosts' half and proceeded to run straight at the defence. Proving too quick and powerful for the approaching central defender, Costa sped past him and, gathering his balance after almost stumbling and as another defender approached, he rifled his shot low and hard past the helpless keeper. With fifty-eight minutes played however, Costa reacted to being brought down near the halfway line by kicking out at his aggressor, earning himself an instant red card in the process. Although his team would cling on for victory, Costa's fourth dismissal of a professional career still in its infancy only served to illustrate how much he still had to learn.

A win and two draws followed as Albacete continued their topsy-turvy league form. Following a 3–1 defeat away at Levante, who had come back down to the second division following two seasons in the top flight, Costa found himself benched for the visit of two-time La Liga winners Real Sociedad. Spending their second season in the second tier of Spanish football having previously not been outside of the top division since 1966–7, the team from the city of San Sebastián in the Basque Country fell behind after just sixteen minutes in south-east Spain before Marquitos, a future team-mate of Costa, equalised just after half-time. But in the final minute of the penultimate match of 2008, with both teams seemingly heading for a share of the spoils, Costa, on as a second-half substitute, anticipated an awful piece of decision-making from a Sociedad defender to latch onto his wayward header and display neat control before tucking past the keeper. The goal gave Albacete all three points and an early Christmas present for under-pressure coach Juan Martínez, who celebrated with an emotional hug from his match-winner.

Costa, having already clocked up seven yellow cards and one dismissal in fifteen matches since the start of the season, missed the last game before the festive break, a heavy 3–0 reverse at the hands of Las Palmas, through suspension. The defeat meant Albacete headed off for Christmas lying fourteenth in the league table, seven points clear of the relegation zone but six points adrift of the promotion places. There was still an awful lot to play for with twenty-five matches of the forty-two-game season to go.

In the first game of 2009, it looked like Albacete were heading for a defeat to a Zaragoza team who were looking to bounce back up to the top flight at the first attempt following their relegation the previous season. Being led by Costa's future captain at Atlético Madrid, Gabi, Zaragoza led by a single goal with just six minutes remaining when Merino won the hosts a penalty. Up stepped Costa and cool as you like, he stroked the ball home, sending the goalkeeper in the wrong direction to earn his team a well-earned point. Two defeats followed before Costa inspired Martínez's men to three points on the road for only the third time up until that point of the season, against Alavés.

Firstly, Costa, having minutes earlier somehow missed an open goal from only yards out, put the ball into the net from an identical position to put his team one ahead. And in the second half, after receiving the ball inside the opposition half, Costa fed a lovely through ball into the path of his forward partner Toché, who made no mistake to put Queso Mecánico (Albacete's nickname) into a comfortable 2–0 lead to wrap up the points. A defeat and a draw followed before the team squandered a two-goal lead to draw a thrilling match 3–3 with promoted Girona. Costa scored from the spot but the dropped points left Albacete an unlikely eleven points behind the promotion places and just five points above the drop zone.

Costa tucked away another penalty, his eighth goal of the season, in a 2–0 home win over Castellón before a second red card of the season on the Canary Island of Tenerife in a 1–1 draw saw him suspended for three matches as punishment for his poor disciplinary record of eleven cautions and two dismissals. Already on a yellow card, with the defender in possession deep in his own half and going nowhere, Costa bizarrely kicked out at his opponent, presumably in frustration at the stalemate, to receive his marching orders for the fifth time in his short career.

Upon his return from three matches kicking his heels on the sidelines, and with Albacete resigned to another season in the Spanish second division, Costa, back in the starting eleven, looked on as Elche took an early lead in their fixture in the south-east. However, six minutes later Albacete were back on level terms when forward Jonathan Soriano profited from Costa's tenacious work on the edge of the area to chip Willy Caballero in the Elche goal to pull Albacete level. And with just over twenty minutes remaining, Costa celebrated his return to the team with the winning goal when his unusual diving header at the back post trickled over the line to give Martínez's men the points.

The goal, Costa's ninth since arriving from Atlético on loan, would prove to be his last for the club and although Albacete lost five of their remaining ten games following Costa's return from suspension, the team comfortably avoided any relegation concerns by finishing eight points clear of the dreaded drop zone, whilst also a massive thirty points outside the promotion places. After two seasons plying his trade in the Spanish second division, Costa returned to Atlético Madrid hoping to test himself on a bigger stage. Little did he know that Atlético would be happy to grant him his opportunity – but not maybe in the way he had expected.

# CHAPTER 4

# A STEP UP IN CLASS

'The difference between a successful person and others is not a
lack of strength, not a lack of knowledge, but rather a lack of will.'
Legendary former American football coach Vince Lombardi
on what it takes to succeed in life

After spending two seasons out on loan learning his trade
in the Spanish Segunda División, Diego returned to the
Vicente Calderón in the summer of 2009 to find a new man
at the helm. Out had gone the Mexican Javier Aguirre after
nearly three years in charge.

Sacked somewhat harshly the previous February with
Atlético lying in seventh position in La Liga, Aguirre, who
had led the club to a fourth place finish in 2007–8 and with
it a first Champions League place qualification since 1996–7,
was replaced by former Atlético goalkeeper Abel Resino in the
hot seat.

Yet for Diego, it was the end of his time in the Spanish
capital. Or so he thought. In two years, he had failed to
make a single appearance for Atleti. And now he was being

ushered out of the door as part of a deal to bring Real Valladolid's highly rated Argentinian goalkeeper Sergio Asenjo to Madrid. It was understandable, however. In rising to a fourth-place finish under Resino, Atlético's prolific front duo Diego Forlán and Sergio Agüero had hit the back of the net forty-nine times between them with Forlán earning the Pichichi Trophy for the division's top goal scorer in the process. However, although they were willing to let Costa move on, the club smartly insisted on inserting a buy-back clause into the deal. If he could exert himself well in his new surroundings the prospect of a swift return to the Spanish capital would be a definite possibility.

On the other side of the city meanwhile, Atlético's eternal rivals Real Madrid responded to Barcelona winning a domestic double and the Champions League by splurging upwards of £200 million on players of the calibre of Kaká, Xabi Alonso, Karim Benzema, Raúl Albiol and Álvaro Arbeloa, and perhaps most significantly Portuguese superstar Cristiano Ronaldo for a world record fee of £80 million from Manchester United. They meant business. And their spending power under returning President Florentino Pérez only served to highlight the widening gulf of wealth and power between Spain's big two and the rest of the clubs in the country. Barca reacted to Real's money-no-object recruitment drive by procuring a star signing of their own, Swedish maverick Zlatan Ibrahimović arriving from Internazionale to partner Thierry Henry and Lionel Messi in attack in exchange for Samuel Eto'o and a reported £50 million-plus.

For Costa though it was yet another new start, another new club, his fifth in only four seasons since arriving in Europe.

But unlike the previous three campaigns this year, in this one he would be rubbing shoulders with some of the world's finest talent and also some of the toughest defenders with Real Valladolid competing in Spain's Primera División. It was his chance to prove to Atlético that he could cut it in one of the world's best leagues.

His new home, for the season at least, was Valladolid, a city of over 400,000 people 190 kilometres north-west of Madrid in the Castile and León area of the country. A wine-producing region and a big player in the automotive industry with Renault España based there, the city's football club Real Valladolid had escaped relegation to the Segunda División on the last day of the previous season with a 1–1 draw against Real Betis to ensure another campaign of top flight football at the Estadio Nueva José Zorrilla.

However, the build-up to the new La Liga season was overshadowed by the shock death of Espanyol's newly appointed captain Daniel Jarque. The twenty-six-year-old passed away following a heart attack on the Catalan club's pre-season tour to Florence in Italy, which led to a huge outpouring of tributes as the football world reacted in shock to another footballer's death following the horrific on-field collapse and subsequent death of Sevilla's Antonio Puerta two seasons before during his club's opening league match of the 2007–8 campaign.

Valladolid strengthened modestly during the summer as they looked to avoid a third season in succession needing a positive result on the last day of the campaign. Former Manchester United flop Manucho arrived from Hull City to strengthen the team's forward options along with highly rated

Real Madrid youngster Alberto Bueno, who signed a five-year contract, but after his arrival from Atlético Costa was to miss out on his new employer's first match of the season, an away trip to Andalusia in southern Spain to face Almería.

The teams played out a dull scoreless draw to earn both clubs a point apiece, but following an international break that saw Costa's home country Brazil achieve qualification for the 2010 World Cup finals in South Africa, Valladolid head coach José Luis Mendilibar named the Brazilian in his starting line-up for the visit of Unai Emery's financially stricken Valencia to north-west Spain. This was it. His time had arrived, his long-awaited debut in Spain's top flight against the might of Valencia, La Liga champions twice under Rafael Benítez earlier in the decade. It would be a tall order though. Valencia were still able to field the likes of David Villa, David Silva and Juan Mata in their starting line-up despite the club's well-publicised financial woes.

And it wasn't to prove a great start for Costa and his team-mates as an early defensive mistake allowed Los Che to go 1–0 up through Silva. A goalkeeping error at the other end allowed Valladolid to equalise with half an hour played but Valencia were back in front four minutes later when Villa, the poacher supreme, turned home Pablo Hernández's cross. Mata increased the lead once more on the stroke of half-time and Villa added his second ten minutes after the restart to end the game as a contest. Manucho's consolation goal reduced the deficit but ultimately it was to prove a disappointing debut for Costa in the lilac and white stripes of La Pucela despite completing his first ninety minutes of top division football.

Valladolid bounced back the following weekend to beat

Zaragoza on their travels, Costa announcing himself with a fantastic assist as his driving run to the byline and cross was turned home by Marquitos to give Los Blanquivioletas (another of Valladolid's nicknames) a 1–0 lead after only four minutes. The hosts would draw level after twenty-six minutes but when Costa's looping header back across goal caused panic in the hosts' six yard area, midfielder Sisi pounced to seal the points for Mendilibar's men, their first victory of the new campaign.

Valladolid hosted Osasuna in midweek and twenty-five minutes in, Walter Pandiani, the veteran Uruguayan forward nicknamed 'El Rifle' stunned the home crowd with a fabulous 35-yard volley to put Osasuna ahead. Just after the half-time restart, however, Costa, having only entered the action from the bench despite impressing in the victory over Zaragoza, notched his first goal for his new club. Receiving the ball out wide on the left, he ghosted past the retreating centre half showing an impressive turn of speed before slipping the ball inside the near post with aid of a very slight deflection. He'd done it, his first goal in top-flight football. However, a defensive howler from a free kick with eighteen minutes remaining allowed Osasuna to slip home a winner and render Costa's goal meaningless.

A crushing 3–0 defeat in Palma to Mallorca followed and the team allowed a 2–1 advantage to slip when Iker Muniain's goal with thirteen minutes left rescued a point for ten-man Athletic Bilbao, in the process breaking the Spanish top-flight record for youngest-ever goal scorer at the age of just 16 years and 289 days. The Basque outfit had led early on through Markel Susaeta, only for his colleague Ustaritz to see red for pulling Costa down, with the big man clean through on goal. But having been denied a clear goalscoring opportunity once already, Costa wasn't to be denied again as he grabbed the leveller on the hour, cleverly working his way into space before firing his shot into the bottom corner. His second goal for the club and an early birthday present to himself just three days before his twenty-first birthday. Valladolid edged ahead with fifteen minutes left before being reduced to ten men themselves and witnessing Muniain create history against them. The draw left the hosts lying a lowly sixteenth in the league after six matches but also just a point adrift of the more illustrious Atlético Madrid on five points.

Costa returned to Madrid one week later for the first time since moving north to take on the daunting task of facing Manuel Pellegrini's expensively assembled Galacticos at the Bernabéu. It would be his first head-to-head clash with Real's central defensive partnership of Sergio Ramos and Pepe, a duel in its infancy that would become more and more physical in years to come upon his eventual return to Atlético. And it didn't take Los Blancos long to get into their stride as Raúl, making a record 711th appearance for Real, celebrated the landmark occasion with an exquisite back heel to put the hosts ahead fourteen minutes in. Real's legendary captain doubled the lead four minutes later with Madrid threatening to run riot only for new signing Nauzet Alemán to curl home a delightful free kick past Iker Casillas to silence the home supporters and halve the deficit.

A stunning strike from Marcelo with the last kick of the half extended their lead to two, but capitalising on a poor pass from Xabi Alonso, Costa's clever pass through Pepe's legs allowed Marquitos to bend his shot around Casillas with the outside of his left foot. Unfortunately for La Pucela though, Alonso atoned for his earlier error to put Gonzalo Higuaín one-on-one with the Valladolid goalkeeper and the Argentine forward's neat chip finally made the game safe for Los Merengues. Costa came close to pulling one back for the visitors late on but after rounding Casillas following a crafty run in behind Pepe, the Portuguese international and Ramos combined to prevent his goal-bound shot crossing the line. Valladolid had lost the match but the team from Spain's north-west had given a good account of themselves while Costa, unperturbed by the quality of the opposition and having caused Real's defence all manner of problems, gave notice of what was to come in the future.

Over in the red-and-white half of Madrid meanwhile, there was yet another managerial change as Atlético President Enrique Cerezo, who had previously said that head coach Abel Resino would 'continue for the rest of the season – it would be madness to change our coach now,' had a change of heart. Having just seen Los Rojiblancos humiliated 3–0 by Osasuna in Pamplona, leaving the club in La Liga's bottom three, in addition to a crushing 4–0 Champions League defeat at the hands of Chelsea, Cerezo had seen enough. Out went Resino. And after countless rumours and near-farcical conjecture over his successor, Cerezo appointed former Real Madrid right back Quique Sánchez Flores to the poisoned chalice. He became the sixteenth head coach at the Vicente Calderón since Atleti last won the title in 1996 under Radomir Antić.

Welcoming high-flying Deportivo La Coruña to the Estadio Nuevo José Zorrilla a week later, Mendilibar's charges produced one of their best performances of the season to subject their opposition from the northern port of Galicia to a 4–0 beating. Nauzet scored his second and third goals in two games to put Valladolid two ahead before Costa smashed home his third goal since arriving to the obvious delight of his team-mates following some indecisive defending from Depor. Manucho almost added a fourth, hitting a post after good build-up play from Costa but the hosts added gloss to an emphatic win late on when Haris Medunjanin clipped home from the edge of the box.

Costa was rested for the Copa del Rey first-leg clash with Mallorca in midweek but with the sides all square at 1–1, Valladolid's number 22 emerged from the substitutes bench to once again show his killer instinct in front of goal, turning his man and firing home to give Valladolid a 2–1 advantage ahead of the return in Palma two weeks later. Medunjanin was on target for the second league game in a row four days later when his spectacular effort right at the death earned Valladolid a valuable away point at Espanyol. A frustrating goalless draw at home to troubled Xerez followed, while elsewhere Costa's former employers Atlético continued their terrible form with a 3–2 home defeat at the hands of Real in the Madrid derby to lie a lowly eighteenth in the league table. Three days later the trip to the Balearic Island of Mallorca for the Copa del Rey second leg resulted in Valladolid exiting the competition on away goals following a slender 1–0 defeat.

After an eleven-day break for the players due to the latest round of international fixtures, Valladolid travelled to Valencia to face Villarreal looking to continue their decent run of form in the league. Before the match, both teams paid their respects to former Villarreal and Mexico striker Antonio de Nigris who had died from a heart attack six days previously. Six days prior to di Nigris' death, the sporting world had once again been in shock as details of German international goalkeeper Robert Enke's suicide emerged.

After dominating the opening forty-five minutes at El Madrigal but with just one goal from Brazil striker Nilmar to show for their efforts, El Submarino Amarillo, who had been struggling themselves for form in the league, were three goals to the good within twelve minutes of the second half restart. Costa's fellow countryman Nilmar doubled Villarreal's advantage before Giuseppe Rossi added a third. Costa, never one to acknowledge a lost cause, grabbed a consolation on the hour latching on to an under-hit back pass with an impressive turn of speed before rounding the advancing goalkeeper and sliding the ball home, his fourth goal in ten matches and a respectable return thus far.

Los Blanquivioletas hoped to get back to winning ways in their next fixture against fellow strugglers Tenerife. The team from the Canary Islands were locked on the same points as Valladolid going into the match and with Costa looking dangerous from the referee's first whistle, it was the home side who broke the deadlock. Displaying brute strength to wrestle himself free of his marker near the halfway line, Costa powered through on goal before showing poise and composure to slide the ball under Tenerife's advancing goalkeeper. Costa, having an inspired match, then threaded a lovely ball through for a team-mate in the box and after being felled, Uruguayan midfielder Néstor Canobbio side-footed the resulting penalty home for a 2–0 lead at the interval.

With the home side still dominating, five minutes after the restart Costa climbed highest from a corner to display another impressive side to his game, heading decisively past the keeper for 3–0. Game over? Not quite. Unbelievably, three dreadful pieces of defending allowed Tenerife to score three goals in the last twenty-seven minutes for a share of the spoils as Valladolid contrived to throw away a seemingly unassailable lead. For Costa, having notched a brace for only the second time in his professional career, his team-mates' lackadaisical defending had cost him and the club a valuable victory and two points in the fight to move away from the relegation zone. However, with six goals from twelve league matches and an impressive strike rate of one in two, on a personal note Costa was already proving that his early promise at Albacete and Celta was no fluke. He was a force to be reckoned with. Atlético, with that buy-back clause in their possession, couldn't fail to be impressed by the twenty-one-year-old's progress.

A trip to the far south-west of Spain to Andalusia and a difficult clash with third-placed Sevilla, the country's oldest football club, lay in wait for Valladolid next. Once again it was Costa at the forefront of the action when his terrific cross from the left enabled Manucho to head La Pucela into a shock lead just past the half-hour point. But after being reduced to ten men shortly after taking the initiative, a foul on Sevilla's dangerous winger Jesús Navas allowed Brazil international centre forward Luís Fabiano to equalise from the penalty spot right on half-time. Sevilla applied heavy pressure in the second period but with Fabiano guilty of spurning numerous opportunities, Valladolid withstood the onslaught to secure a well-earned point at the intimidating Ramón Sánchez Pizjuán.

## A STEP UP IN CLASS

The team spurned the chance to pull clear of the drop zone in the next game when fellow strugglers Málaga left the Estadio Nuevo José Zorrilla with a 1–1 draw. The cold weather in the north-west led to the last game before the Christmas break against Sporting Gijón being played out in icy conditions. And with Costa proving a constant thorn in Málaga's side whilst spurning a number of chances throughout the match, Valladolid recovered from a one-goal deficit to pinch a vital win with another last-minute winner from Medunjanin to extend their unbeaten run to four matches.

However, Valladolid's decent pre-Christmas form came to a crashing halt upon the league's resumption in early January when a 1–0 defeat on the road to Getafe and a 4–0 home thumping at the hands of Flores' vastly improved Atlético saw the club slump towards the drop zone. It had been a golden opportunity for Costa to impress new Atlético boss Flores, but with his team under-performing it was the attacking trio of Agüero, Forlán and José Antonio Reyes who took the opportunity to shine instead.

A 1–1 draw away at Racing Santander preceded the expected 3–0 drubbing at the hands of Lionel Messi and his still-unbeaten Barcelona team-mates in Valladolid before the team allowed another winnable match at home to struggling Almería to slip through their hands. The team managed just a point in a 1–1 draw as Costa's dry spell in front of goal extended to nine matches despite his best efforts. Yet if Costa thought he was going through a bad spell, two days after Valladolid's drubbing at the hands of Barca, his own troubles on the field would be put into context in the worst possible way.

## DIEGO COSTA: 'THE BEAST'

The football world was left in a state of shock once again when it was broadcast that Paraguay's prolific forward Salvador Cabañas of Club América in Mexico had been shot in the head in a nightclub incident. He would never play football to such a high standard again. A goal drought was nothing to be overly concerned about in the light of such desperately sad news from across the Atlantic Ocean. But with Valladolid resting just a point above the relegation places, and without a win since the final match of 2009, Mendilibar paid the price for the club's recent poor form with his job before the team's daunting trip to face Valencia at the Mestalla.

Ahead of the match on the Mediterranean coast, the board promoted 'B' team coach and former Valladolid winger Onésimo Sánchez González to the role of first team head coach. However, his reign began in predictable fashion as Los Che completed a league double over their visitors thanks to goals from Éver Banega and La Liga top scorer David Villa. Against Zaragoza the following Sunday, Costa's goal drought finally came to an end after ten long matches when he bravely headed home from close-range to put Onésimo's men in charge. However, a superb solo goal from Chilean centre forward Humberto Suazo denied Valladolid's new man in charge a first victory, causing the team to slip further into the mire in nineteenth position in the league table.

An eleventh draw of the season followed away in Pamplona against Osasuna before a 2–1 home defeat at the hands of Mallorca saw La Pucela precariously positioned in the bottom three and four points adrift of safety, Costa having been denied an equaliser right at the death by the visiting goalkeeper's agility. Meanwhile, Costa's idol as a child growing up in

Lagarto, Ronaldo, now in the twilight of an illustrious career and turning out for Corinthians back home in São Paulo, announced his decision to retire at the end of the 2011 season: 'I've renewed for another two years and they will be the last of my career.'

Two further defeats at the hands of Athletic Bilbao in the Basque Country and a 4–1 hammering at home to top-of-the-table Real Madrid pushed Valladolid closer to the drop before Onésimo finally saw his team emerge victorious in his seventh match in charge, a 2–0 victory over 1999–2000 La Liga champions Deportivo in La Coruña. The victory gave hope that Los Blanquivioletas could beat the drop. However, their hopes of doing so took two massive knocks when Costa was red-carded in the very next game, a 0–0 draw at home to Espanyol. His dismissal for an innocuous looking stamp on defender Dídac Vilà on the touchline, his sixth in only four seasons as a professional was followed by an inexcusable 3–0 reverse for the team at the hands of relegation-doomed Xerez, a match Costa would miss due to suspension.

With the team lying five points from safety and still in nineteenth position, their survival hopes took yet another dip when Villarreal left Valladolid with all three points following a comfortable 2–0 victory. It was a defeat that would cost Onésimo his job after only nine matches in charge, the board concluding his record of only one win in nine would almost certainly lead them back to the Segunda División unless they acted swiftly. With Onésimo gone, the board opted for experience in the battle to escape relegation, hence the appointment of the wily, much-travelled former Spain supremo Javier Clemente, Valladolid's third head coach of the season.

And the fresh approach appeared to do the trick. Valladolid reacted to his arrival firstly with a goalless draw away at fellow relegation candidates Tenerife, before an impressive 2–1 home win over Sevilla thanks to a header from Costa, his ninth of the season, and a curler from Manucho to give the hosts renewed hope of beating the drop. The new coach was having the desired effect as Valladolid again kept a clean sheet to win a point on the road at seventeenth-placed Málaga. With only five matches remaining to save themselves La Pucela were fighting for their lives and a 2–0 win in Gijón the following Sunday increased the optimism around the club as Clemente instilled a toughness into the team that saw the club's leaky defence conceding fewer goals than at any time during the season.

Clemente's men kept a fourth clean sheet in his five matches in charge as they drew 0–0 at home to Getafe. However, with only three matches left and two of them against mid-table Atlético Madrid and title-chasing Barcelona, it was a case of two points dropped against Getafe rather than one point gained. Costa returned to the Vicente Calderón in midweek with his team looking for a win or a draw at the very least to preserve their hopes of survival. And it was Valladolid who made all the early running with Costa causing his former employers all sorts of problems on the left of the visitors' attack, nearly creating a goal for Manucho, before the Angolan striker was denied a clear penalty soon after. Costa continued to cause havoc in the Atlético defence with his direct and powerful running but with Manucho proving wasteful it was Flores' team who eventually took advantage of the visitors' profligacy in front of goal to win a hard-fought match 3–1.

The defeat, Clemente's first since taking charge, meant Valladolid went into the match against fellow strugglers Racing Santander needing all three points to take their relegation scrap right down to the wire and their last match against Barcelona at the Camp Nou. The home team did little to settle the nerves inside the Estadio Nuevo José Zorrilla, however, as Los Verdiblancos took a first-half lead. But after being rallied by Clemente during the break the team fought back to score from a corner before Nauzet successfully dispatched a penalty to win the match and move them out of the drop zone and into sixteenth position for the first time since match day 20.

And so it would all be decided in Barcelona's gargantuan cathedral of football, the Camp Nou. Valladolid needed an unlikely win or at the very least a draw to retain a chance of staying up. But crucially Barcelona also needed to win with Real Madrid breathing down their necks for the La Liga crown. Madrid travelled to the Costa del Sol to face relegation-haunted Málaga at their hosts' boisterous and packed La Rosaleda Stadium. Any slip up from Barca would allow their fierce rivals from the Spanish capital to steal in and pinch their crown if they could dispatch Málaga and condemn their hosts to relegation.

It was a tense situation for all parties concerned. After just four minutes Valladolid missed a golden opportunity to draw first blood when Manucho hit his shot straight at a defender with Víctor Valdés exposed following a poor back pass. And two minutes later with Costa's aggression and power causing Valdés and the Blaugrana defence problems galore, Baraja, who had scored the first goal in Gijón the week before, saw his long-range effort fly just wide of the post. Valladolid were giving it a real go. But after settling down and peppering La Pucela's goal incessantly with a number of shots and Messi uncharacteristically missing a one-on-one with Valladolid's keeper Jacobo, Barca took a fortunate lead with twenty-seven minutes played when Pedro's cross-cum-shot was sliced into his own net by Valladolid defender Luis Prieto. Things were beginning to look ominous.

Within four minutes Barca were two goals to the good, Pedro coolly sliding home Messi's inch-perfect through ball. Valladolid were staring down the barrel. Barcelona were heading for their second successive title and twenty-first in total. Two second-half goals from Messi sealed their triumph and the Pichichi trophy for the prolific Argentine for the first time. Barcelona were champions once again. For Valladolid the season finished in dejection and disappointment as Málaga's improbable 1–1 draw with Real Madrid and Racing Santander's 2–0 win over Sporting Gijón subjected Clemente's men to relegation after only two seasons back in the top flight.

For Costa there was the disappointment of relegation in his first season playing top division football. But having endeared himself to the fans of Valladolid with nine league goals in thirty-six games and nine yellow cards and one red to boot, there was no doubting he had given his all for the cause. Although still on a learning curve, his raw power, infectious enthusiasm and will to win had won him many new friends in north-west Spain, but had he done enough to persuade new Atlético boss Quique Sánchez Flores to activate the buy-back clause and take him back to the capital? Or would he be spending another season with Valladolid down in the Segunda División? Only time would tell.

# CHAPTER 5

# WINDOW OF OPPORTUNITY

'Who's this bag of shit you've brought us?
Some bloody eyes you've got.'
Atlético scout Javier Hernandez recalls an Atlético-supporting
friend's reaction to seeing Costa during his first season.
He may have a different opinion today.

When Quique Sánchez Flores arrived at the Vicente Calderón in October 2009, Atlético Madrid were a club in crisis. Sitting in the relegation zone after seven matches under his predecessor Abel Resino and with the club also out of the Champions League, Flores turned Los Colchoneros around to secure a satisfactory if unspectacular ninth place finish in La Liga and a first trophy since Radomir Antić's double-winning team of 1995–6.

A 2–1 extra time victory, courtesy of two Diego Forlán goals, over Roy Hodgson's Fulham in the Europa League final had given them their first European trophy since winning the now defunct European Cup Winners' Cup final way back in 1962. They had also reached the final of the Copa del Rey, or Spanish Cup, falling at the last hurdle as Sevilla triumphed

2–0 in Barcelona's Camp Nou. But despite doing well in the cups, the club needed to perform better in the league to try and propel themselves back into the lucrative Champions League.

After impressing the Atlético hierarchy with his performances in north-west Spain for Valladolid, the club did indeed exercise their €1 million option to bring Diego Costa back to the Vicente Calderón in the summer of 2010. However, he was under no illusions as to his standing in Flores' squad. After performing for their respective countries at the summer's World Cup finals in South Africa – won ultimately by Spain – Atlético still boasted Sergio 'Kun' Agüero and World Cup golden boot winner Forlán as their first-choice strike force. Costa would play a back-up role. Nothing more. But he was at least being given a chance to be part of the squad at the club he had joined over three years earlier.

Having retained the services of all their star players whilst adding promising left back Filipe Luís from Depor, the highly rated midfielder Fran Mérida from Arsenal, utility player Mario Suárez from Mallorca and the tough Uruguayan Diego Godín from Villarreal to shore up La Liga's fifth worst defence from the previous season, Atlético were looking much stronger ahead of the forthcoming campaign. Hopes were high that Flores could keep the momentum of the previous campaign going. With Agüero and Forlán to score the goals and a reshaped defence, Flores had raised the hopes and expectations of Atleti's fanatical supporters. And Costa wanted to prove himself a capable cog in the Atlético wheel when given the opportunity.

Over on the white half of the city meanwhile, following a trophy-less season under Manuel Pellegrini, despite all the millions of euros spent the previous summer, José Mourinho, the new man in charge after Pellegrini's dismissal, sanctioned the departures of Real legends Raúl and Guti, whilst welcoming Benfica's electric left winger Ángel Di María and German schemer Mesut Özil to the Spanish capital. Over in Catalonia, champions Barcelona also waved goodbye to two stalwart players as Yaya Touré departed for megabucks Manchester City while Thierry Henry's three-year stint at the club ended as he set off on a new journey of discovery, joining New York Red Bulls in the MLS. To replace him, Spanish hotshot David Villa was recruited from Valencia to try and ease the burden of goal scoring carried by the magical Lionel Messi.

Atlético kicked off the new season with a morale-boosting 2–0 victory over Internazionale in the UEFA Super Cup final in Monaco. Three months earlier, Inter, in Mourinho's last game in charge of the Nerrazurri stewardship, had defeated Bayern Munich in the final of the Champions League across town at Real's Santiago Bernabéu stadium. However, with Mourinho having departed Lombardy to take control at Atlético's arch-rivals Real, it was Flores and his men who would go on to collect the first trophy of the season courtesy of goals from José Antonio Reyes and Agüero. For Costa it was a landmark first career medal, despite spending the whole ninety minutes on the bench as an unused substitute.

Three days later, however, and over three years after first signing for Los Rojiblancos, Costa did finally pull on the famous red and white striped shirt for the first time as he made his long-awaited debut as a second-half replacement against Sporting Gijón. With Atlético three goals to the good with just over twenty minutes remaining, Flores sent Costa on in place of Forlán, who had already helped himself to a brace of goals to put Atlético firmly in charge. Costa couldn't muster a debut goal but Atlético wrapped up a crushing 4–0 opening day victory courtesy of a spectacular strike from Portuguese winger Simão, another substitute, to send the adoring Vicente Calderón fanatics home delighted and optimistic of a good season to come. Things were already starting to looking rosy on the red and white side of Madrid.

Following his twenty-minute cameo appearance against Gijón two weeks earlier, Costa was back on the bench for the trip north to face Bilbao at the intimidating San Mamés stadium. And his chances of displacing either Agüero, just four months his senior, or the prolific Forlán on the team sheet looked slim at the time, especially given Forlán's early-season form, which saw him combine with his Argentine strike partner to open the scoring in Bilbao, his third goal in two games. Forlán had started the season where he had left off the previous season, scoring goals for fun.

On the hour mark, however, Costa's chance arrived albeit in unfortunate circumstances. After a horrible challenge on Agüero led to the squat Argentine marksman being stretchered off with a leg injury, Costa was summoned from the bench by Flores. With Forlán's solitary strike still proving the difference between the two teams and the game in the balance, Costa helped Atlético to seal the win as the away team launched a counter-attack directly from a Bilbao corner. Picking the ball up in his own half, Costa ran purposefully at the retreating defenders before releasing an inch-perfect pass to Simão, whose shot was parried out by the Bilbao goalkeeper straight to Portuguese midfielder Tiago, who strode in to head home a simple header with twelve minutes remaining. And although the Basque outfit pulled one back late in the game through Fernando Llorente, Atlético held on to take their place at the top of the La Liga table with two league wins from two, a great start to the campaign and an encouraging initiation to life in Madrid for the young Diego.

A disappointing start to the club's aspirations of retaining their Europa League crown followed as Atleti stumbled to a disappointing 1–0 defeat at the hands of Aris Saloniki in Greece, Costa playing the second half of a frustrating match for the visitors. A second defeat in three days followed when Barcelona arrived in Madrid looking to make amends for their shock 2–0 defeat at the hands of newly promoted Hércules the previous weekend. Messi slotted home early on to put Barca ahead, only for Raúl García to head home Simão's corner to make matters all square. However, seven minutes later centre half Gerard Piqué was on hand to smash home a Messi corner to end Atlético's 100 per cent record as Barca escaped the capital with a hard-fought win.

Having replaced Agüero for the last thirty-eight minutes of the Barcelona clash, Costa was promoted to the first eleven for the trip to table-toppers Valencia at the Mestalla in midweek, his first league start as an Atlético player. It would be a proud day for his family back home in Brazil. At the age of just twenty-one, here was Diego leading the famous Atlético Madrid attack in the absence of the injured Agüero alongside Diego Forlán, top scorer at the summer's World Cup and the Pichichi winner just over a year ago. It was the stuff of dreams for him. And it looked like being a day to remember for Costa as Simão's first-half goal looked to have given the visitors all three points only for Los Che to grab an equaliser and a share of the spoils with seven minutes of the match remaining.

Agüero had recovered sufficiently to take his place on the bench for the visit of Zaragoza to Madrid four days later. But having impressed his manager throughout the draw at Valencia, Flores kept faith with Costa and the big man repaid his manager's confidence in him with his first goal for the club twenty minutes into the match. A nice move down the left allowed new signing Filipe Luís to break into the opposition box and his neat centre allowed Costa to slide in ahead of his marker to put Atlético in front. It was Costa's moment, one to savour, his first goal for Los Indios and the game's only goal, the winner at the Calderón in front of his own supporters. What a day, what a moment to celebrate for Diego and his family. All the hard work and spells out on loan had been worth it. Now here he was scoring the winning goal in a Spanish top division match for one of Europe's biggest clubs. Atlético held on to win the game despite Reyes' red card leaving the team down to ten men for the last thirty minutes.

The team attempted to get their Europa League defence back on track against Bayer Leverkusen in midweek with Costa starting his third match running for the hosts. But it was the German side that would notch first only for Simão to cancel out the lead from the penalty spot as Atlético earned their first point of the group stage. A difficult trip to face Sevilla at the ever-intimidating Ramón Sánchez Pizjuán followed. And after falling 3–0 behind to goals from Álvaro Negredo, Diego Perotti and Frédéric Kanouté, although Costa was able to pull one back with a fine finish from a tight angle just twelve minutes after entering the fray as a second-half substitute, for the second season in a row Atlético were defeated 3–1 by their hosts in Andalusia.

Looking to get back to winning ways after the defeat in southern Spain's bullfighting capital, Flores, clearly delighted by his young striker's promising form, promoted Costa after his goalscoring entrance against Sevilla back into the starting line-up for the visit of Getafe on 16 October. Even Forlán, without a goal in four league matches, had to play second fiddle to the man in form as Flores demoted the Uruguayan to the substitutes' bench. And get back to winning ways they did. Atlético took the lead thanks to another excellent strike from Simão, this time direct from a free kick, to lead at the interval. And with the match still on a knife edge, latching on to Valera's centre, Costa easily poked home from close range to make the game safe with his third goal in four league starts. He was justifying Flores' faith in him and his impressive goalscoring exploits had helped to propel Atlético into fifth position in the table after seven matches, just four points adrift of city neighbours Real at the summit.

Forlán returned to partner Costa in the club's next Europa League outing against Norwegian league champions Rosenborg at the Calderón. Diego Godín put the hosts ahead with his first goal since arriving from Villarreal in the summer, before the club's returning fans' favourite, Agüero, only on the pitch in place of Forlán for sixty seconds slid home the second to double Atleti's advantage. And with twelve minutes remaining, Costa got in on the act, profiting from a slick one-two with Agüero to intelligently loop his header over Rosenborg's advancing keeper and wrap up Atlético's first win in the group stage with his fourth goal in five matches.

## DIEGO COSTA: 'THE BEAST'

In Agüero's absence, and with Forlán having lost his scoring touch of late, Costa had taken full advantage of the opportunities afforded him by Flores to stake a claim for a role within the team. And having proved to his coach he was able to get himself into the positions to score goals, with Agüero back to full fitness and restored to the starting eleven for the trip to Valencia to face Villarreal, it was the master Forlán and not the apprentice Costa who would have to settle for a seat on the bench at El Madrigal.

With just two minutes on the clock, Costa and Agüero showed promising early signs of a developing partnership when the Brazilian sliced the hosts' defence open with a cute pass for the Argentine. Agüero stroked the ball past the advancing Diego López in the Villarreal goal and into the net only for the referee's assistant to rule out the goal for a narrow offside. Seven minutes later the hosts made Atlético pay when Nilmar slipped Cani in and the midfielder's finish evaded David De Gea in the Atlético goal. Atlético were denied a blatant penalty on the stroke of half-time when Agüero, once again at the centre of the action, was clearly felled in the area only for the referee to inexplicably blow his whistle for half-time rather than a spot kick, to Agüero and his team-mates' angry protestations. Seven minutes after the interval, Villarreal rubbed further salt into Atlético's wounds when former Manchester United youngster Giuseppe Rossi dribbled his way through the visitors' defence to increase the lead to two goals and regain second spot from Barcelona in the league table.

Having lost the Copa del Rey final against Sevilla the previous season, Atlético got their 2010–11 assault on the cup underway against minnows University of Las Palmas de Gran Canaria. Agüero and Costa's budding partnership continued as Diego Maradona's son-in-law helped himself to a brace of goals and Costa notched his fifth senior goal to help Atlético to a straightforward 5–0 victory. But Costa was back on the bench for the home match with Almería on Halloween, Forlán and Agüero being reunited up front for the hosts. However, despite Agüero putting Atlético ahead, Almería equalised on the stroke of half-time and the match ended 1–1.

Having been benched for the league game the previous weekend, Flores restored Costa to his starting line-up for the trip to chilly Trondheim to face Rosenborg in the latest Europa League group fixture. And after the Norwegians' second-half equaliser of Agüero's opening goal had threatened to deprive Atlético of a much-needed win in a tight group, Tiago's wonder goal from 30 yards late on wrapped up the tie in the Rojiblancos favour ahead of the huge trip across town to the Bernabéu the following Sunday evening.

Flores opted for experience over youthful exuberance as Forlán retained his place alongside Agüero in the team ahead of Costa for the short journey over the river to face Real in the day's standout fixture. Atlético went into the game without a win over their bitter rivals in ten years and that statistic would continue as Ricardo Carvalho and Mesut Özil gave Los Merengues a lead with twenty minutes played. Atlético had limited opportunities to get back in the match with Forlán striking a post in the second half, but it was Real who looked the more likely to add to their lead as they comfortably regained their place at the top of La Liga from Barcelona.

Following the disappointment of the derby defeat, Atlético

returned to Copa del Rey action in midweek to face University of Las Palmas de Gran Canaria. Costa, having experienced his first taste of Madrid derby action as a late substitute the previous Sunday, was back in the team for the second leg of the cup with Atlético holding a five-goal lead from the first leg. However, after conceding the first goal to the tiny club from Gran Canaria with twenty minutes played, Costa's day got a whole lot worse when five minutes before half-time he was shown a straight red card for elbowing an opponent in retaliation. His petulant actions wouldn't threaten Atlético's progress as the team clawed back the deficit to draw the match 1–1, but it showed a lack of maturity to Flores that would result in him being used sparingly for the rest of the calendar year.

With Costa now sidelined by suspension, Atlético swept past Osasuna 3–0 at the Calderón in their very next match, Forlán helping himself to a brace and Agüero completing a straightforward victory. After sitting out the win over Osasuna, Costa found himself back on the bench for the trip to San Sebastián to face Real Sociedad at the Anoeta Stadium. And once again it was the Forlán–Agüero partnership that would come to the fore as Atlético recovered from a goal down to score four goals in the final twenty minutes to seal a clinical 4–2 away win in the Basque country.

Costa saw his opportunities limited to a series of late substitute appearances in the following matches as Atlético lost three games on the bounce, ending their involvement in the Europa League and succumbing to disappointing La Liga losses at home to Espanyol and away at Levante. The team got their campaign back on the right track with a 2–0 win over Deportivo La Coruña before an impressive 3–0 victory on the road at Málaga saw them consolidate sixth place in the table. But for Costa it was proving to be a testing time. His red card in the Spanish Cup had seen him seemingly lose the faith of the head coach Flores. And with Forlán and Agüero resurrecting their partnership with some important goals in recent weeks, it was hard to see how he would force his way back into the team barring injury. However, Costa displayed maturity beyond his years when quizzed about having to wait his turn behind the club's star duo:

> I knew that I was going to have a tough time starting. But I think that I took advantage of the minutes I had. I left everything on the pitch. I was aware that Forlán would recover from his scoring drought. Kun is also in fine form. They form a great duo and have been playing together for many years. I'm going to keep working to take advantage of my opportunities. The team is what's important.

An injury to Forlán in the very next game, the first leg of the Copa del Rey last 16 tie with Espanyol gave Costa his chance to force his way back into Flores' good books. Entering the fray after fourteen minutes, Costa helped Atleti to overcome Reyes' first-half red card to win the tie 1–0 thanks to Simão's well-finished penalty. In Forlán's absence, Costa retained his starting position for the scoreless draw with Racing Santander, the 1–1 second leg cup draw at Espanyol and a 4–1 thrashing at the hands of Hércules in Alicante, but with Forlán fit again, the Uruguayan replaced Costa for the 3–1 defeat at the hands of Real in the Copa del Rey quarter final first leg.

## DIEGO COSTA: 'THE BEAST'

With Agüero now missing through injury, Costa was afforded his last start for over two months as Atlético went down 1–0 in the Bay of Biscay to Sporting Gijón. In the next ten matches and with Costa sidelined by Flores, Atlético embarked upon a disastrous run of form which saw them exit the cup at the hands of Real 4–1 on aggregate and only collect a meagre eight points from a possible thirty in La Liga, ending the run with yet another demoralising 2–1 defeat at the hands of old foes Real at the Calderón. The chances of Flores' team achieving their Champions League qualification target were already dead and buried with eight matches of the season still to play.

Having made a twelve-minute appearance in the defeat to Real the previous weekend and with Agüero out injured once again and Forlán dropped to the bench, Costa was recalled to the starting line-up for the difficult trip to Pamplona to face Osasuna at the El Sadar Stadium. Just past the half-hour point it had looked as if Atleti's disastrous run of form was set to continue when the hosts took the lead. However, they hadn't reckoned with an inspired Costa. Having played only a handful of minutes recently, all from the bench during Atlético's poor run of form, Costa set about proving to Flores that he could be an asset to the team. Eight minutes after going one behind, Costa stole in off the shoulder of the last defender latching onto new recruit Juanfran's superb pass (Juan Francisco Torres Belén was signed in January from Osasuna) before expertly curling the ball over the despairing keeper's dive to put Atlético level. It was a proper striker's finish.

And Costa put Atlético 2–1 ahead just past the hour, sprinting clear of the home defence before coolly sliding the ball beyond the reach of Osasuna's advancing goalkeeper. And within two minutes his first brace for the club became his first hat-trick when he sped onto another through ball to nutmeg the hapless Osasuna keeper to make it 3–1. It was not only his first hat-trick for Atlético, it was his first hat-trick anywhere as a professional footballer. The match ball was his to keep for the first time in his career. A proud moment for the boy from the tiny Brazilian town in the middle of nowhere. Reyes missed a penalty which would have added gloss to the scoreline before Osasuna pulled one back themselves from the spot late on to revive hopes of a comeback. But Atlético held on for the win as Costa enjoyed the adulation of his team-mates and Flores, who praised his young striker after the final whistle:

We planned a very aggressive match up front, and it went well. We wanted to play as far away from our goal as we could and we achieved that. We staved off the first wave from Osasuna and then we imposed our style. Against these battle-hardened opponents, Diego knows how to play well. He holds them off and when he takes off he's stronger than his defenders. Everything pointed to it being an encounter like this. He exceeded the expectations we had for him both in goals and actions. He did more than we thought he would.

After his stunning hat-trick the previous weekend, there was no way Flores could drop Costa for the home match against Real Sociedad at the Calderón, and so it played out as Forlán once again found himself benched in favour of the twenty-two-year-old Brazilian. Agüero had recovered to take his place alongside Costa at the head of the Atlético attack and within twelve minutes of the kick-off the Brazilian forward's intuitive back-heel enabled left back Filipe Luís to put Atlético into an early lead.

And on the stroke of half-time the Rojiblancos were two goals to the good when Reyes' wonderful trickery on the left was rewarded by Mario Suárez's calm finish. This was more like the Atleti the crowd were yearning to watch, not the team of the last two months. Late on Agüero added the icing on the cake to make it 3–0 and keep Atlético in the hunt for the final Europa League qualifying place awarded to the club finishing seventh in the league table. Ahead of the clash with fellow Europa League chasers Espanyol, Costa spoke to the club website expressing his happiness with his current form whilst also revealing how much he was learning from Agüero and Forlán:

I'm working just as hard as other weeks to try and be amongst those chosen. Then the gaffer is the one who decides who plays. I was also playing well at the beginning of the season with a good scoring streak. Things have gone well for me, but Forlán is a tremendous player and could return to the starting eleven at any time. The coach has his ideas. There are changes from one game to another in the starting line-up, and I wouldn't be surprised if I wasn't amongst those selected. I've worked hard all week, but I don't feel like I'm the starter. I'm learning other things with respect to those I learned at my previous side, Real Valladolid. I'd like to continue on at Atlético next year, but I don't know what's going to happen. I'm very happy with the ovation I received last week from the crowd. I hadn't played in a long time and getting that acknowledgement from my fans was really nice, as they felt I played well, and hopefully I can keep this good form. It's much harder to play at Valladolid than here because Kun and Forlán are really good. I'm learning a lot from them, as they're both amazing players.

Atlético travelled to Barcelona for the match with Espanyol at the Estadi Cornellà-El Prat in high spirits having secured maximum points from their last two league games. And the match in Catalonia got off to the best possible start for the visitors when Koke capitalised on a terrible defensive error to put Atleti 1–0 ahead inside just two minutes. Dani Osvaldo drew Mauricio Pochettino's men level before half-time with a deflected shot from inside the box, but Atlético recaptured the lead when Agüero raced clear before exquisitely chipping the goalkeeper to put Flores' men back in charge. However, Espanyol wouldn't be denied as Osvaldo once again scored from a well-placed header to ensure the race for Europa League qualification would go down to the wire.

Los Colchoneros welcomed Levante to the Calderón the following Sunday aiming to exact revenge on the visitors for the 2–0 reverse imposed on them earlier in the season, and retribution is exactly what they earned as summer signing Elias cracked home a stunning free kick after nineteen minutes to set them on their way. Levante drew themselves level from the penalty spot before the break but after the interval the irrepressible Agüero smashed the hosts back in front from long range. Costa earned his team a penalty of their own, which Agüero despatched with typical aplomb, and a late own goal gave Atlético a comfortable 4–1 victory as the team's recent revival continued.

A solitary strike from Atlético's golden boy Agüero away at Deportivo La Coruña gave the visitors their fourth win in five games before the team's recent good form came to a crashing halt as Manuel Pellegrini's struggling Málaga outfit left the Calderón with an unexpected and crushing 3–0 victory to keep their hopes of survival alive. Costa would miss the club's second defeat in a week as they crashed to a 2–1 defeat to Racing Santander on the road in Cantabria, northern Spain. And although he would be back on the bench for the club's last two matches of the season against Hércules and Mallorca, the Brazilian youngster would play no further part as the club secured Europa League football for the following season thanks to two wins from two, the second against Mallorca courtesy of an Agüero hat-trick.

The season had been a steep learning curve for Costa. Although he had shown he could provide a useful option to the coach in the absence of either Agüero or Forlán he hadn't fully convinced the coach he should be a regular starter. In fits and starts he had shown he could score goals, but could he be relied on week-in week-out? However, would Flores still be at Atlético following another massively disappointing season? Would Atlético be able to retain their star man Agüero? Would Forlán, who had fallen out with Flores on a number of occasions throughout the season, stay at the Calderón? It would prove to be a massive summer for the future of Diego Costa.

## WINDOW OF OPPORTUNITY

As Javier Hernandez, the scout who recommended his signing to Atlético recalled, Costa may not have had the best of first seasons in the Spanish capital, but the promise was there for all to see, even if not everyone was able to see it in those early days:

In Diego's first season, the Calderón booed and whistled him. Once an Atleti-supporting friend told me: 'Who's this bag of shit you've brought us? Some bloody eyes you've got!' I responded: 'You're wrong. He's a good player. You've got to let him grow.' No one remembers that now.

# CHAPTER 6

# COMEBACK KID

*'It is not the size of a man but the size
of his heart that matters.'*
Former heavyweight boxing champion
of the world Evander Holyfield

When Diego Costa arrived back in Madrid for pre-season training in the summer of 2011, he did so to be welcomed not by Quique Sánchez Flores who had afforded him his debut as an Atlético player the previous season, but by a new incumbent of the poisoned Atleti chalice. Flores had departed the Vicente Calderón circus having seen his team finish a disappointing seventh during the 2010–11 campaign. Having finished a dismal thirty-eight points behind eventual champions Barcelona, the team claimed the final Europa League qualifying position on offer but missed out on the pre-season goal of Champions League football. Failure to get beyond the group stages of the Europa League – a competition his team had won during his first season in charge – coupled with Copa del Rey elimination by city rivals Real Madrid all resulted in Flores' contract not being renewed.

## DIEGO COSTA: 'THE BEAST'

Replacing him in the seemingly ever-revolving hot seat would be a familiar face to the long-suffering supporters of Los Colchoneros. Gregorio Manzano Ballesteros had been in charge of Atlético once before. During his previous tenure in the 2003–4 season, his team had also finished the La Liga campaign in seventh position. But back in 2004 such a placing only guaranteed the occupiers a place in the ridiculous and now defunct Intertoto Cup. He departed at the end of that campaign and following spells with Málaga and Mallorca took Sevilla to a fifth-place finish in 2010–11. Sevilla finished the season two places above Flores' team. However, with Sevilla, Athletic Bilbao and Atlético Madrid all tied on the exact same number of points, fifty-eight to be exact, the Andalusian's and Basque's superior head-to-head record over Atlético saw Flores' team placed bottom of the three teams in seventh.

Manzano arrived at the Calderón tasked with persuading the club's star players to remain in the Spanish capital and give him the chance to help them achieve their goals. However, with Atlético having under-achieved once again in the previous campaign, missing out on Champions League football in the process, and with the vultures circling over the club's star players preventing the club's major assets moving on to pastures new was always going to prove a forlorn hope.

Atlético's star player and fans' favourite Sergio Agüero departed Madrid for Roberto Mancini's FA Cup winners Manchester City in the English Premier League. His strike partner Diego Forlán, who had suffered a serious dip in form and numerous alleged fall-outs with the coach during Flores' second season in charge, flew the nest to join Coppa Italia winners Internazionale. And David De Gea, the club's outstanding young stopper, who had graduated from Atlético's academy system, became the most expensive goalkeeper in British football history when he signed to replace the retiring Edwin van der Sar at Sir Alex Ferguson's nineteen-times English champions, Manchester United.

Replacing the front duo of Agüero and Forlán would be Colombian hotshot Radamel Falcao, who arrived on the back of scoring thirty-eight goals in forty-two appearances on his way to inspiring FC Porto to a Portuguese league and cup double and Europa League glory. Also arriving in Madrid would be talented playmaker Arda Turan from Turkish giants Galatasaray, Thibaut Courtois, the highly rated Belgian goalkeeper on loan from Chelsea, midfield general Gabi who would go on to become club captain, Adrián López, a forward from Deportivo La Coruña, and Eduardo Salvio, the Argentinian midfielder from Benfica.

For Costa it looked like being decision time. With Falcao the obvious number one striker at the club following his stunning €40 million arrival, would Costa get a look-in during the season? Also, not being in possession of a prized European passport, it looked like his days at the club were numbered. He hadn't done himself any favours in the popularity stakes with his coach either, reporting back for pre-season training in Madrid three days late. In addition, Atlético already had three non-EU nationals on their books with only three permitted to play each week, and with Falcao, Salvio and the centre half Miranda almost guaranteed their positions within the team, Costa, still only twenty-two, would have to look elsewhere in search of regular action, be it on loan or permanently.

And with the transfer window drawing to a close at the

end of August, it looked to all as if he had found a new home. A move to the Turkish Süper Lig and Beşiktaş was drawing to a conclusion, with only a medical standing between him and a departure from Atlético after only one full season at the Calderón. However, in his final training session with Atleti before heading to Istanbul, Costa crumpled to the floor having ruptured the cruciate ligament in his right knee: the move was off. Costa was going nowhere. And not only would he be deprived of first team football, he would be out of action for at least six months. Disaster.

In his absence, with the club adjusting to life under yet another new manager and with a number of new players to bed into the squad, Atlético got off to an uninspiring start as they drew their first match of the season 0–0 at home to Osasuna before following it up with defeat at the hands of Valencia at the Mestalla. Five goals in two games, including a hat-trick against Racing Santander, saw Falcao capture the hearts of the loyal Atlético fans. However, a crushing 5–0 defeat courtesy of a Lionel Messi hat-trick at the Camp Nou followed in the very next game as Atlético's early-season form continued to fluctuate wildly.

Despite comfortably qualifying for the knockout stages of the Europa League from a group containing Celtic, Stade Rennais and Udinese, a further five defeats in La Liga, including heavy reversals at the hands of Real Madrid, Athletic Bilbao and Espanyol, saw Manzano walking a fine line with the club's trigger-happy board.

And when the team failed to overturn a 2–1 deficit from the first leg of their fourth round Copa del Rey tie with Costa's former loan club from the second division, Albacete, the board acted swiftly and ruthlessly to remove Manzano from his position. Out of the cup and sitting a disappointing eleventh in La Liga following only five victories and seven defeats, Atlético were lurching from crisis to crisis and Costa, still recuperating from his injury, could do nothing to help.

Replacing Manzano as the latest in a long line of coaches to take the impossible job was one Diego Pablo Simeone. 'El Cholo' as he is widely known, arrived just before Christmas 2011 and was a popular choice in the red and white half of Madrid, having captained the double-winning team to glory in 1996, the last time Atlético had won the domestic league or cup in Spain. Simeone had cut his teeth in management in his native Argentina, impressing with an 'Apertura' or opening championship success as coach of Estudiantes in 2006 and a 'Clausura' or closing championship victory as supremo of Buenos Aires giants River Plate in 2008. Following a short, unsuccessful spell in charge of Catania in Italy and Racing Club of Argentina, Simeone arrived in Madrid charged with the challenge of succeeding where so many before him had failed, breaking the stranglehold of Real and Barcelona.

With Costa side-lined until the start of February, Simeone began his tenure in the hot seat after the Christmas break with three wins and a draw from his opening four games in charge, Falcao increasing his total for the season to fourteen goals by the end of January. But with Costa now back to fitness, a decision on his next move had to be made. Would Simeone give him the opportunity to impress with game time at Atlético? Unlikely, with Adrián, Koke and Arda Turan providing the bullets for the deadly Falcao to fire.

And so he was on the move once again. This time though it

wouldn't involve uprooting and a move away from the city as he landed up at Rayo Vallecano, a club based in the capital in the neighbourhood of Vallecas. It was his fourth stint out on loan since arriving at Atlético in early 2007. But this time there was something different about him: he looked more powerful, more physical despite his relative lack of fitness. And starting his first match for Rayo from the bench away at Zaragoza, with the team trailing by a single goal at half-time, head coach José Ramón Sandoval threw his new acquisition into the fray to partner future Swansea striker Michu at the head of the visitors' attack.

After Rayo had squandered a great opportunity to equalise from the penalty spot, it was Costa who rose highest to head home superbly and drag his new team level with fifteen minutes to play. Six minutes after Costa's equaliser and with the time running out, Michu pounced to side foot a lovely finish into the net to wrap up all three points and give Costa a winning debut at Zaragoza's La Romareda stadium.

Having impressed after coming on as a replacement against Zaragoza, Sandoval promoted Costa to the starting eleven for the club's next game at their quaint home ground, the Campo de Fútbol de Vallecas. And after Michu had rolled them into a half-time lead, Costa once again showed his prowess in the air when he headed home a free kick to give Rayo their second win in succession. It was a great start to life in Vallecas for Costa, and after the frustration of missing the first five months of the season through injury, he was clearly delighted to be making up for lost time, whilst showing off his range of qualities to new Atlético coach Simeone at the same time.

Against Levante in the team's next game, Costa rose highest

for the third match in a row to head home powerfully and give Rayo a 2–1 lead after sixty-two minutes, and one minute later the big man showed he was equally adept with his feet as he fired his team into a two-goal lead with just under half an hour remaining. An exhilarating match would finish 5–3 to Los Franjirrojos, with Costa's predatory instincts inspiring his new team to another great victory. Meanwhile over at the Calderón, Simeone, witness to three consecutive draws from his new charges, surely couldn't fail to be impressed by his big man's efforts out on loan, especially with Atlético only managing to yield one goal from their three matches.

A solitary strike from La Liga's top goalscorer Cristiano Ronaldo proved enough for José Mourinho's men to return home across the city victorious despite a tough challenge from Rayo. The result, not a disaster by any stretch of the imagination against Los Merengues, who were ten points clear at the top of the division, left Rayo and Costa just one point behind his parent club Atlético following their own narrow 2–1 defeat at the Calderón to Barcelona.

Sandoval's men got straight back to winning ways in their next fixture as they welcomed struggling Racing Santander to Madrid. The visitors' woes continued when with just three minutes played their goalkeeper Toño saw red after clattering dangerously into Costa who was clean through on goal. In an incident reminiscent of goalkeeper Harald Schumacher's disgraceful charge at Patrick Battiston during the 1982 World Cup semi-final between West Germany and France, Costa on this occasion was lucky to be able to get back to his feet and play out the remaining eighty-seven minutes.

Incredibly, despite being down to ten men following Toño's

early dismissal, Racing actually raced into a two-goal lead within the first half an hour. Sandoval, clearly unhappy with his side's shocking efforts, made two changes before the interval bringing forwards Piti and the veteran Raúl Tamudo on as his team went in search of a way back into the game. And on the stroke of half-time Michu cut the deficit with a well-placed header before smashing Rayo level from close range just past the hour mark following dangerous work from Costa on the left. Soon after, Tamudo proved he had lost none of his goalscoring instinct despite his advancing years when he glanced home a lovely clipped cross from Costa out on the right, before Rayo's on-loan star, putting in a man-of-the-match shift, played a nice one-two with Piti to allow Sandoval's other inspired substitution to wrap up the game in the home team's favour.

Costa, perhaps luckily for him, missed out on the 5–1 drubbing at the hands of Espanyol in Catalonia but returned to inspire Rayo to a 3–0 win over Real Betis the following weekend as the club continued their impressive recent home form. Costa's deft through-ball got the ball rolling after the second half restart to enable Emiliano Armenteros to finish calmly and put Rayo into the lead. And Rayo's dangerous Brazilian added the second himself twelve minutes from time when he again illustrated his increasing influence from set plays to head home, before Tamudo wrapped up an impressive 3–0 victory in injury time.

Rayo slumped to a second heavy away defeat in a row when they travelled to Andalusia to face Champions League-chasing Málaga. Costa had actually fired the visitors ahead from the penalty spot five minutes into the match, but despite winning another late penalty which was successfully put away for his team, Manuel Pellegrini's impressive team Málaga emerged victorious, 4–2. Further losses followed for Rayo as they tumbled to a 2–0 defeat at home to Villarreal, before the team again took a beating on the road, this time from Real Sociedad who embarrassed them 4–0 in a one-sided drubbing.

A brief respite for the team arrived in the shape of a 6–0 thrashing of Osasuna at the Campo de Fútbol de Vallecas. And Costa scored one of the best goals of his career to date when cutting in from the left side of the pitch he curled a beautiful shot into the top far corner of the net. The goal gave Rayo an unassailable 4–0 lead before half-time before Sandoval watched his team add two further second-half goals to treat the fans to their biggest win of the season and avert thoughts of possible relegation for ninety minutes.

However, another heavy defeat lay in wait for Rayo the following weekend when they conceded four on the road for the fourth match in succession, this time at the hands of Valencia. With seventy-two minutes played, Rayo trailed 2–0 but Costa, never one to give up, combined with strike partner Michu to pull one back, his eighth goal in just eleven games, only for Valencia to score two late goals of their own to continue their own pursuit of Champions League football at the other end of the league table.

Across the city a Ronaldo treble led Real Madrid to yet another victory over Costa's parent club Atlético at the Vicente Calderón to open up a four-point gap at the top of La Liga over second-placed Barcelona. It meant the Rojiblancos had now gone thirteen years without a win over their fierce rivals, unacceptable to their passionate supporters. With

Rayo's indifferent form sucking them towards a relegation scrap, Costa under the rules of his loan agreement was forced to miss out on the home clash with Simeone's Atleti. He would have loved to have been out there showing Simeone what he was missing, but in his absence Rayo lost again, this time to Falcao's well-taken second-half breakaway goal.

Things were beginning to look bleak for the Franjirrojos. Freefalling down the league, the only thing standing between them and an instant return to the Spanish second division was the equally poor form of the teams below them in the table. An ill-tempered 2–1 loss at Sporting Gijón followed the derby loss to Atlético, before Barca came to Madrid and taught Rayo a footballing lesson, subjecting their abject hosts to a 7–0 thumping. A fifth defeat in a row away at Mallorca followed, and not even two goals from Costa, the first from the penalty spot and the second a late tap in, could salvage anything from Rayo's trip to Seville as they flew home having lost 5–2 in the knowledge that anything other than a victory at home to Granada the following weekend would probably be insufficient to rescue them from relegation.

With José Mourinho's Real Madrid already crowned La Liga champions, breaking Barcelona's three-year stranglehold on the title, the real excitement going into the season's last round of fixtures centred around the teams at the bottom of the division and the question of who would succumb to the dreaded drop. Costa's goals and assists had, in his short time at the club, given the Rayo supporters reason to be hopeful. But with any one of four teams still looking over their shoulders, it was a tense time. Rayo, Zaragoza, Granada and Villarreal were all in the mix.

With the matches approaching their conclusions and Zaragoza seemingly safe leading 2–0 away at Getafe, the pressure at Rayo's small but atmospheric stadium was building. With their match still goalless against Granada, and Villarreal tied 0–0 with Costa's owners Atlético, a return to the Segunda División looked an increasingly likely possibility. Rayo needed to score, otherwise they were goners. Villarreal could even afford to lose and they would stay up so long as Rayo didn't win.

And so it came to pass. Atlético, aware that Málaga were now leading their match against Sporting Gijón, which would in turn deny them any hope of Champions League qualification, netted in the closing seconds against Villarreal, Falcao the inevitable scorer. It made no difference though, Rayo were still going down if they couldn't find a breakthrough. But incredibly, with the seconds ticking down and the referee starting to check his watch at the Campo de Fútbol de Vallecas, following all manner of squandered gilt-edged chances, Raul Tamudo, on as a late throw of the dice, headed Michu's rebound off the bar into the empty net from a yard out.

The goal sparked hysteria in the ground as Rayo's coaching staff, players and fans rejoiced at their achievement. Having been promoted to La Liga the previous season for the first time in ten years, Rayo were safe. Villarreal meanwhile, who only six years before had been Champions League semi-finalists, were relegated. The final whistle in Vallecas witnessed a mass pitch invasion such was the joy of their nerve-shredded supporters. Costa rejoiced with his team-mates and the fans. He had given so much to the cause with his ten goals in just sixteen matches. And he had proven once and for all he could cut it in Spain's top division.

Sandoval described him as 'the best striker in the world for what I want to do', while Atlético's feared fitness trainer Óscar 'El Profe' Ortega looked on in awe at the club's forward who had recovered from knee surgery to become one of La Liga's most dangerous strikers:

> It's not logical that he recovered from such a serious knee injury, went to Rayo and scored ten goals when he'd had basically no training whatsoever. I couldn't believe my eyes. You can't explain this, no matter how many books you read. I asked him what work he'd done as a kid and he told me 'nothing', that he'd come from the street. There are no limits to his strength. He's a bull.

Ortega was certainly impressed, but the man he needed to impress the most was the man at the helm of Atlético, 'El Cholo'. And it wouldn't be long before he would find out whether there was a future waiting for him across the city at the Vicente Calderón or not.

# CHAPTER 7

# THE REAL DIEGO

'Success is no accident. It is hard work, perseverance,
learning, studying, sacrifice and, most of all, love of what
you are doing or learning to do.'
Brazilian legend Pelé outlines his method for success

Diego Costa arrived back at the Vicente Calderón stadium in the summer of 2012 confident that his impressive exploits out on loan at Rayo Vallecano the previous season would earn him a chance to impress the new man in charge of Atlético Madrid, Diego Simeone.

Simeone had assumed control of the under-achieving club from the working-class suburbs of Madrid back in November 2011 following the dismissal of the previous short-term incumbent Gregorio Manzano. His appointment was universally popular, especially with the club's long-suffering fans. He had, after all, been club captain the last time Atlético's fans had anything major to shout about. Way back in 1996, Atlético, with Radomir Antić at the helm and Simeone his trusted lieutenant on the field, finished the season as champions of Spain and Copa del Rey winners. Never before in the club's long history had they achieved the double. However, that one season of glory, unbeknown at the time, would be the club's last silverware for fourteen years. And during those years in the wilderness the club and its fans had to endure the added heartache of seeing their cross-city rivals Real win the league title five times and Europe's premier competition, the Champions League, on three occasions.

When Atlético did finally end their long wait for a trophy in 2010, winning the newly formed Europa League, the heir to the UEFA Cup, many looked upon it as a sign that the club were finally back. However, league performances continued to disappoint, leading to the eventual appointment of Simeone. '*El Cholo*' was a no-nonsense guy who took no prisoners as player, and that mentality was the exact thing the club was in desperate need of. A leader who would put the team first, who wouldn't tolerate any egos undermining his authority, and most important of all to the fans, somebody who could help Atlético challenge Real's dominance over them – somebody who could build a team to compete. Of course, during his first season back at the club, they had won a second Europa League title in three years, but what the fans craved more than anything was success in La Liga, and a long-awaited win over Real. They had been waiting since 1999 to taste victory over their great rivals. It had been too long.

Having helped Rayo Vallecano to earn an unlikely La Liga reprieve with his goals in the last four months of the 2012–13 campaign, Costa was quietly optimistic about his future prospects at his parent club. Ten goals in sixteen games had inspired Rayo to avoid relegation back to the Spanish second division. Surely, Simeone, who was about to start his first full season in charge of Atleti would have been impressed by what he saw happening across the city?

Well maybe. But with Radamel Falcao still an Atlético player having plundered thirty-six goals in all competitions during his first season at the club, and Simeone a confirmed fan of Adrian López – less prolific but no less hard working – Costa was in for a shock. Ahead of the new season, Simeone, as quoted in *World Soccer* magazine, told Costa: 'You're probably not going to play much but we will train you as if you were going to play.'

It was disappointment for the Brazilian, but it only spurred him on to prove Simeone wrong. And when Atlético allowed Argentine midfielder Eduardo Salvio to part company with the club to head to Benfica ahead of the transfer window closure, an opportunity presented itself. With Salvio's departure, the ruling which allows teams to play only three non-EU nationals meant there was now one space free, assuming Miranda and Falcao would still occupy the other two slots. Costa trained like his life depended on it in pre-season, prompting Simeone to comment: 'I wanted to kill him. He was doing these amazing diagonal movements. He was flying, absolutely flying. I told him, "Your characteristics suit our play. I do not have any commitment to specific players: what I want is to win."'

Encouraged by his head coach's kind words, Costa could sense a long-awaited chance to finally feel important at Atlético. However, his opportunity wasn't to present itself straight away. The team got their campaign underway with a trip to face a Levante team who had finished the previous season in sixth place in La Liga. It was their highest finish ever in La Liga and presented them with European football for the first time in the club's history. Levante away was always tough. And when the line-ups were announced, Costa's name was nowhere to be seen as Simeone chose to start the campaign with Adrián supporting main goal threat Radamel Falcao in attack. He didn't even make the bench. Looking to get the season off to a good start, Atlético suffered a setback with just five minutes on the clock when ex-Liverpool youngster Nabil El Zhar fired the hosts into the lead. The advantage was short-lived, just seventeen minutes in fact, as Turkish magician Arda Turan jinked past his marker before rifling an unstoppable shot into the roof of the opposition net to draw Simeone's men level. The season had started with a satisfactory if unspectacular start.

Eight days after their opening-day point, Atlético welcomed Athletic Bilbao to the Vicente Calderón for the first home match of the season. It was just over three months since the two clubs had squared up to one another in Bucharest for the Europa League final. Atlético had prevailed 3–0 that night to win the trophy and Bilbao arrived in the working-class region of Madrid looking to exact revenge on their hosts.

However, that man Falcao, who had scored two goals in the Romanian capital to inspire Atlético to European glory, would again prove the scourge of Bilbao as his hat-trick guided the Rojiblancos to a 4–0 win in front of their delighted supporters. Costa came off the bench with twenty minutes remaining for his first appearance of the season, but three days later he would spend the full ninety minutes rooted to his seat when for the second time in his Atlético career he collected a European Super cup winner's medal without even kicking a ball in anger. Falcao once again proved what a wonderful goal scorer he was, notching a stunning hat-trick, his second in just four days, to give Atlético a 4–1 victory over European Champions Chelsea in Monaco.

Having only tasted twenty minutes of action from the opening three fixtures, Costa earned a call-up to the starting eleven for the visit of Rayo Vallecano after the international break in mid-September. Chosen ahead of Adrian to partner the prolific Falcao up front, Costa couldn't have wished for a better start when after twenty-nine minutes he illustrated his capabilities to Simeone and the watching Calderón as he teased his marker before pulling the ball back to Mario Suárez who stroked home to make it 1–0. After the break, Costa combined with Falcao on the right to help himself to another assist as he set up a simple tap in for Koke to double Atlético's advantage.

Two minutes later the home team made it three when Costa combined with Juanfran in a carbon copy of the second goal down the right, to give Arda the simplest of finishes to seemingly end the match as a contest. After Falcao increased the lead to 4–0 from the penalty spot, Costa gave way for new signing Cristian Rodríguez but following his exit from the field Simeone's men almost conspired to throw away their four-goal advantage as Rayo fought back to score three times in the last eight minutes. However, despite their indecision at the back, Atlético held on, just, to make it seven points from a possible nine.

Four days later Costa helped the Rojiblancos get their Europa League campaign off to a winning start in Israel as the team triumphed 3–0 over Hapoel Tel Aviv. Costa again proved a thorn in the side of the opposition as, firstly, his tenacity up front in shielding the ball from his marker allowed him to set up Rodríguez for the opening goal. The big man, displaying a new lease of life since his recovery from injury the previous season, then made it two just before half-time when, making one of his trademark runs off the shoulder of the last defender, he latched onto a perfect through pass to round the goalkeeper and roll the ball into an empty net. Raúl García added a third to wrap up the result from a corner.

Atlético's promising early-season form continued the following weekend when Diego Godín strode through the middle of the park before clipping home to put the hosts 1–0 ahead against Real Valladolid. It was a goal both Falcao and Costa would have been proud to have scored and set Atleti on the road to another victory which Falcao would confirm from the spot after Costa was felled in the penalty area. Atlético made it four league wins in a row in Seville three days later with a 4–2 victory over Real Betis despite twice falling behind during the match.

Betis went 1–0 up before the half-hour mark before Falcao, the poacher supreme, was on hand to turn home Raúl García's centre to square the match up just two minutes later. Betis regained the lead going into the break when Juanfran's block on a cross eluded Sergio Asenjo, who was starting in place of regular keeper Thibaut Courtois in the Atleti goal. The match turned in Atlético's favour after the restart when Betis defender Damien Perquis hauled Falcao to the floor to earn himself a red card and a penalty for the visitors. 'El Tigre' confidently tucked away the resulting spot kick to draw Los Colchoneros level and put himself top of the La Liga scoring charts, before

Costa, only on the pitch for two minutes as a replacement for the injured Colombian, popped up unmarked at the back post to side foot home a knock-down from Suárez and put Atleti ahead for the first time in the match with his first league goal of the season. Los Verdiblancos were reduced to nine men late on following Joel Campbell's second yellow card of the night, and with the hosts pushing forward in search of an equaliser Raúl García found himself unmarked at the back post to turn home in the dying seconds.

In Falcao's absence, Costa began the game with Espanyol in Catalonia leading the Atlético attack, and in their star striker's absence, Raúl García, the scorer of so many important goals for the club found himself in acres of space to head Simeone's men to their fifth victory in a row and keep them within two points of Barcelona at the top of the table. A 1–0 victory over Czech team Viktoria Plzeň ensured Atlético's 100 per cent record in the Europa League stayed intact and the following weekend, with Falcao having recovered from his injury in time for the visit of Málaga to the Calderón in early October, the Colombian wasted little time getting back in the groove as he headed the home team in front with just six minutes played.

Málaga would equalise before half-time through Paraguayan forward Roque Santa Cruz's header, but with the final whistle imminent, pressure from the prowling Falcao forced Málaga defender Weligton to slice the ball into his own net to give Atlético all three points and a share of top spot in La Liga, following Barcelona's 2–2 draw in the first *El Clásico* of the season against Real Madrid at the Camp Nou. Costa sat the match out as an unused substitute. After the team survived several clear-cut chances for Real Sociedad to take the lead in their match in San Sebastián, Costa entered the field of play at the Anoeta stadium just in time to witness a stunning last-gasp winner from his strike partner Falcao's free kick to keep Atlético neck-and-neck with Barca at the top of the table.

Having sat on the sidelines for almost the entirety of the two previous league fixtures, Simeone promoted Costa back into the starting eleven for the club's third Europa League group match against Portugal's oldest professional football club, Académica de Coimbra. And to celebrate his recall following two frustrating matches as a virtual spectator, Costa, following the second-half resumption, latched onto a flick-on from a corner to put the home side ahead with a scissors kick from six yards. Emre Belözoğlu added a second from a beautifully placed free kick to give Atlético another win, their third in the competition, to virtually assure progression from their group to the knockout stages.

With Simeone's men showing a real toughness and togetherness that had been so sadly lacking from so many Atlético teams of the past fifteen years or so, Costa, despite his goal in the Europa League, once again found himself watching from the bench as the Calderón witnessed an eighth league victory in a row with a comfortable 3–1 win over Osasuna courtesy of goals from Miranda, Raúl García and unsurprisingly Falcao, his tenth of the season in just nine league matches. Having played a limited role in Atlético's revival under Simeone thus far, Costa knew he would just have to bide his time and keep training hard in order to win another chance in the first team.

Following a harsh first-half dismissal for a Real Jaén defender in the Copa del Rey tie with the Spanish third division minnows, Costa, back in the starting line-up, punished the opposition to put his team in front with a well-executed penalty. Simeone, looking to take his team much further in the competition than the previous season's embarrassing elimination at the hands of Costa's former loan-club Albacete, saw his team complete a comfortable victory with second-half goals from Adrián and Raúl García to virtually ensure progression to the last sixteen ahead of the second leg four weeks later.

Costa was absent for the club's first defeat of the season, a 2–0 reverse to Valencia at the Mestalla, and also missed out on a first return to Portugal since departing Braga in 2007, when the team suffered their second defeat in a week with a 2–0 loss to Académica de Coimbra, Portugal's third largest city after Lisbon and Porto, meaning qualification for the knockout stages of the Europa League would have to wait a while longer.

Costa returned to the bench for the home league match with Getafe as Atlético sought to get over their blip of two consecutive defeats, and he watched on as an unused substitute once again as goals from Adrián and Arda Turan got the team back to winning ways at the Calderón. But despite starting the next match from the substitutes' roster once again, Costa entered the fray just after the half-time restart to play a big part in the game's winning goal. Sprinting onto Koke's accurate pass in behind the Granada left back, Costa turned goalwards only to be tackled as he aimed to set himself for a shot. However, his quick reaction time enabled him to get back to his feet to feed Koke, who crossed for Arda to put the ball into the opposition net for the game's only goal. And despite Mario Suárez's red card with just over fifteen minutes remaining, the team held on to their lead to guarantee another vital three points as they continued to challenge at the top of the table in their quest to get back into the Champions League.

Meanwhile, back in the Europa League, an early goal from Raúl García proved sufficient for Atlético to confirm their qualification from group B and a place in the draw for the second round of Europe's second competition. And the team won again in their next fixture as they trounced under-performing Sevilla 4–0 at the Calderón. Simeone opted to partner Falcao with Costa from the start of the match, the Brazilian's first league start for nearly two months.

And with twenty-two minutes played and Falcao creating havoc in the Sevilla penalty box, the breakthrough came for the Rojiblancos when Argentinian defender Federico Fazio conceded a penalty and saw red for a tug on Koke, just as the midfielder seemed likely to pull the trigger. Falcao, as usual, put away the spot kick, his fiftieth goal for Atlético, smashing the ball right down the middle to put the hosts 1–0 ahead and firmly in control with a man advantage for the remaining hour or so. Things got worse for the visitors when Fazio's defensive partner Emir Spahić inadvertently turned Arda's ball past his own goalkeeper into the net to give Atlético a 2–0 lead five minutes before the interval. Four minutes later and just a minute before half-time Atlético wrapped up the win when Costa, breaking down the right side of the pitch, beat his marker before cushioning a lovely pass to Koke who stabbed his volley into the corner of the net for 3–0. Atlético eased up on their bedraggled hosts after the break as Miranda added gloss to the victory in injury time ahead of the Madrid derby the next week.

In the build-up to the first Madrid derby of the season across town at the Bernabéu, Atlético safely negotiated the second leg of their Copa del Rey tie with Real Jaén with a laboured 1–0 win over the minnows courtesy of Raúl García's first-half goal. Costa retained his place in the starting line-up alongside Falcao as Atlético attempted to break their twenty-three-match winless streak against their more flamboyant and noisy neighbours. José Mourinho's Real entered the must-win match eleven points adrift of leaders Barcelona and incredibly, eight behind Atlético, who themselves lay just three points behind top spot. The Rojiblancos' supporters entered the Bernabéu for the first time in a long time almost expectant of breaking their thirteen-year hoodoo, which stretched back to 1999. And where better to break it than in front of 79,000 at their rivals' own cathedral of football?

Undergoing a massive transformation in fortunes under Simeone and with the club having made their best-ever start to a La Liga season with eleven wins, one draw and only one loss ahead of the derby, Costa et al saw this as their chance. However, the match itself was to prove a damp squib if ever there was one. Cristiano Ronaldo, almost inevitably, put the hosts ahead to the delight of all *Madridistas* after fifteen minutes, his dipping free kick deceiving Courtois in the Atleti goal to find the corner of the net. However, while Real would add a second to wrap up the match, Ronaldo setting up Mesut Özil to make it 2–0 in the second half, the match would be dominated by the running battle between Los Merengues' defenders Pepe and Sergio Ramos and Atleti's Costa.

The rivalry took on new meaning after an evening of confrontation as Ramos spat at Costa whilst awaiting an Atleti corner. Costa responded by spitting back at his opponent. Both players escaped punishment, the referee having missed their nauseating acts. Yet it says much about Costa's character that after the final whistle he embraced the Spanish international with a congratulatory hug.

Despite the 2–0 loss, Atlético remained five points ahead of their great rivals in second place. In the very next game, a dead rubber in the Europa League against Viktoria Plzeň, with their Czech hosts heading for a 1–0 victory in the ninetieth minute and Costa frustrated after missing opportunities to get Atlético back in the match, the hot-headed Brazilian steamed into a scuffle between Plzeň's David Limberský and youngster Pedro Martín, head-butting the home team's defender to the floor. The indiscretion highlighted Costa's susceptibility to being wound up as the referee gave him an instant red card, earning him a four-match ban from European competition in the process. In the games against Real and Plzeň, Costa had shown his boss Simeone he was not one to shy away from a confrontation. But Simeone would act to calm his volatile yet talented striker, ensuring he wouldn't receive his marching orders during the rest of his time in Madrid.

Simeone kept faith with Costa despite his dismissal in the previous match when he named his team to face Deportivo La Coruña back in Madrid the following Sunday. And his volatile striker put the frustrations of his previous match behind him, when after already going close with a header Costa opened the scoring from Koke's deep corner kick, rising highest to head home at the back post. But from that moment on, after Depor had come close to an equaliser only for the post to deny them, the match would become the Falcao show as Atleti's prolific goal-getter set about putting derby disappointment behind the team and Depor's defence to the sword.

Koke, Atlético's chief creator alongside Arda, created Falcao's first to make it 2–0 before the half-hour point, and after Costa saw another chance go begging, the Colombian who joined Atleti following 72 goals in 87 games for FC Porto, added his second of the match with a fantastic volley on the turn from Arda's throw-in, to put the team three to the good before the interval. He secured the match ball after winning a penalty himself in the sixty-fourth minute and then four minutes later showed incredible desire and bravery to head home his fourth to make it 5–0. And his craving for goals came to the fore for an incredible fifth time with twenty minutes of the match remaining. Latching onto Filipe Luís' pass, he turned his marker inside out before firing past Depor's hapless keeper Daniel Aranzubía to make it 6–0 and become the first player since Real's Fernando Morientes to score five goals in a single match – against Las Palmas back in 2002 – an incredible feat.

Following his stunning five-goal salvo, Simeone opted to rest his top goalscorer Falcao for the midweek Copa del Rey tie against Getafe. And with the team looking to gain a decent advantage ahead of the second leg after Christmas, Courtois twice denied Getafe opportunities to take the lead in front of a sparse crowd at the Calderón before Costa, having lost his strike partner Adrián for the evening to injury, won and converted a penalty to put his team a goal to the good at half-time. After climbing highest from a free kick to head home his second goal of the match only to be harshly denied by the assistant referee's flag, Costa, in the thick of the action all night, then saw his acrobatic scissors kick from a Raúl García knock-down saved by the keeper.

But with the clock ticking down, Filipe Luís turned home to make it 2–0 after Arda's long-range effort rebounded to him off a post, and Costa finally got the second goal his endeavour deserved when cutting in from his favoured position on the left side of attack, he calmly slotted past the advancing keeper to make it 3–0 and put Atlético firmly in charge of the tie with the second leg still to follow after the mid-season break.

With nine goals from their previous two games, Atlético headed to the Camp Nou to face Tito Vilanova's top-of-the-table Barcelona in the penultimate match before the traditional Christmas break, in confident mood and looking to narrow the gap between themselves and their hosts to just three points. Vilanova was still absent from the dugout due to his ongoing chemotherapy for throat cancer and the hosts were led by his assistant Jordi Roura. Things couldn't have started any better for Simeone's men. After applying early pressure on Barca, Atleti were unlucky not to be ahead when Falcao's header rebounded off a post. And after missing another great chance to open the scoring following Koke's quick free-kick, Falcao finally opened it on the half hour when Costa robbed Lionel Messi in the centre circle before releasing his strike partner, who made no mistake this time with a delicious chip over Víctor Valdés.

However, the one-goal lead would prove a false dawn as Vilanova's men recovered from their slow early start to go in at the interval 2–1 ahead after Adriano scored a contender for goal of the season to equalise, before Spain midfielder Sergio Busquets fired home from close range to put the home side ahead. And after the break Barca wrapped up a 4–1 win to re-emphasise their La Liga superiority over their rivals from Madrid. Messi made up for his earlier mistake to increase their lead in the table to a gargantuan eleven points after sixteen rounds of the championship.

Atlético recovered from their heavy defeat at the hands of the league leaders to face Celta Vigo at the Calderón in their final match of 2012 as they looked to finish the first half of the campaign with a flourish. But after toiling to find a breakthrough, Costa, who missed a glorious opportunity from close range before seeing a possible penalty turned down in the first half, was replaced by Adrián after an hour. And it was his stand-in who came up with the goods to break the tension in the stadium when his superb left-footer from 25 yards scorched into the back of the net to win the game 1–0 despite Miranda's late sending off for a second yellow card. The victory ensured Simeone and his team flew back to Madrid safe in the knowledge that they could enjoy the festive period sitting a glorious seven points clear of Real in third position, a marked improvement on years gone by.

After returning from their traditional Christmas holidays, Atlético, missing Arda, Falcao and the suspended Miranda, travelled to the island of Mallorca looking to kick on from where they had left off in 2012. However, despite dominating the match with chance after chance, it took them until the seventy-second minute to finally break down their Balearic hosts when Costa, twisting and turning in the area, saw his attempt pushed out by the Mallorca keeper, but only into the path of Raúl García who finished to put the visitors one up. However, with only three minutes remaining and following a mad scramble in the Atleti defence, Mallorca substitute Kevin found himself in a pocket of space to rifle home the leveller with the aid of a slight deflection off Cata Díaz.

Despite the disappointment of dropping two points in the league, Atleti returned to cup duty three days later to secure their place in the next round of the Copa del Rey against their city neighbours Getafe, a goalless draw proving sufficient to set up a quarter-final tie with Real Betis. The team got back to winning ways with a weekend victory over Zaragoza at the Calderón, goals from defensive midfielder Tiago and Falcao from the spot sealing the points. Over in Catalonia meanwhile, Barcelona's charge towards a twenty-second La Liga title triumph continued to gather pace as a 3–1 win over Málaga gave them a record eighteen wins from their first nineteen games of the season, while Messi took his top division tally of goals to over 200 when he scored a quadruple against Osasuna a week later in a 5–1 walkover of Osasuna at the Camp Nou.

Some wonderful interplay between Costa and Raúl García enabled the irrepressible Falcao to head Atleti into a one-goal lead after just eleven minutes of the first leg of the Copa del Rey quarter-final against Betis. And the advantage became two just past the twenty-minute mark when left back Filipe Luís profited from some dangerous trickery down the left hand side from Costa to give his manager and team-mates some breathing space ahead of the return leg a week later.

Costa found himself back on the bench for the home league clash with Levante the following weekend, but with the hosts leading 1–0 ahead thanks to Adrián's first-half goal, Costa answered Simeone's call on the hour, replacing Falcao after the team's main man pulled up with a hamstring injury. And within a minute of his introduction, Atleti increased their lead to a comfortable 2–0, when Costa combined with Koke before the Spanish international, who joined the club's ranks as an eight-year-old, curled home a marvellous shot from 30 yards into the top corner.

Sitting seven points clear of deadly rivals Real in the league, Atleti ensured progression to the semi-finals of the Copa del Rey four days later when Costa, back in the starting eleven with Falcao sidelined by injury, pounced on some awful Betis defending to put his team on the verge of qualification. Surviving some spirited early pressure from Betis including a stonewall penalty appeal, Costa seized on an unforgiveable mix-up between Betis defender Antonio Amaya and wandering goalkeeper Cato to roll the ball into an empty net and put the tie beyond the team from Seville. Heading into the tunnel for half-time, Costa churlishly thanked Amaya for the gift on the pitch, sparking a mass brawl. Although Betis would grab a consolation in the dying seconds, all of the post-match focus would centre on the half-time incident involving Amaya and Costa. After the full-time whistle Amaya admitted to the assembled press: 'He was very grateful. He was shouting and thanking me for the gift. If my team-mates had not held me back, I would have killed him. That shows what kind of person he is: he has no heart and no shame.'

He may have no shame. But he certainly has heart, and his goal had ensured a place in the last four of the Copa del Rey for Atlético for the first time since losing the final to Betis' fierce city rivals Sevilla back in 2010. In addition, the blue touch paper was smouldering now ahead of the forthcoming league match between the two teams in ten days time. A dismal 3–0 defeat away at Bilbao's San Mamés stadium followed for the club, their first defeat of 2013 and the first since their 4–1 drubbing at the hands of Barcelona back in December.

Costa lined up for the first leg of the Copa del Rey semi-final against Sevilla determined to fire Atlético in Falcao's continued absence into a strong position ahead of the second leg in a month's time. And, in a bad-tempered match that would see three players given their marching orders, Costa proved the match-winner when first he fired home from the spot following Emir Spahić's careless handball under pressure. Then, after Álvaro Negredo also converted from the spot following Godín's dismissal for deliberate handball on the line, Costa once again popped up to turn home a second penalty to give Simeone's team a slender 2–1 lead to take to Andalusia in late February.

With Falcao having recovered from his hamstring strain and ready to take his place back in the team against Betis, Simeone prevented Costa from squaring up to whatever Betis had to throw at him following the previous week's ugly scenes by starting him on the bench. However, with the game ticking by and not a great deal of action occurring, Simeone threw Costa into the fold on the hour. And within five minutes of entering the field of play, it had to be him who made the breakthrough, nodding home from a couple of yards to break the deadlock.

And then things really warmed up. Costa could count himself lucky to only receive a yellow card when a red would have been more appropriate for a dreadful studs-first tackle on Rubén Pérez's calf muscle. And soon after, when Costa's seemingly innocuous challenge on José Cañas left the midfielder rolling around on the floor, the Brazilian could easily have been unfairly dismissed, before Pérez left Atleti substitute Cristian Rodríguez in a heap with a horrible lunge, leading to an ugly mid-pitch brawl as tempers boiled over. With the game approaching its end, Amaya, whilst marshalling Costa in the area as the two players awaited a free kick, left Costa's face awash with saliva, a disgusting act. The referee did nothing but Costa had the last laugh. His team won the game 1–0 thanks to his goal, completing a league double over their visitors in addition to their earlier progress in the Spanish Cup at Betis' expense. After the match, Diego Godín told the waiting press that everyone knew Betis' players would go after his team-mate, while Costa just shrugged off the controversial incidents, insisting he wasn't one to hold grudges: 'There are no scores to settle and no problems. What goes on the pitch stays on it. I don't take it home with me.'

Following the controversial circumstances surrounding Atlético's win over Betis, Costa sat out the dismal 2–1 defeat at the hands of his former loan-club Rayo Vallecano across the city, before watching on helplessly as Atleti somehow proceeded to lose 2–0 at the Calderón in the Europa League first leg to Russian visitors Rubin Kazan despite the away team being reduced to ten men on the stroke of half-time. Atlético got back to winning ways after two losses on the spin when they dispatched another of Costa's former employers, Valladolid, 3–0 in north-west Spain.

Falcao put the visitors in front with eleven minutes on the clock, tapping home from two yards after Valladolid's goalkeeper made a tremendous save to deny Diego Godín. And Costa returned to haunt his former fans when after threatening twice to extend Atleti's lead in the first half, he got his goal eight minutes after the break, finishing clinically from Koke's knock-down before Rodríguez wrapped up the victory in the final minute of the game.

After the final whistle, speaking to the press Costa revealed the importance of the team getting back to winning ways and also his joy at scoring in front of his old Valladolid fans:

> We were good, we pressed well and it was a good win. We came to make a big effort; after the defeat against Rubin we were angry. We worked well and we won the game. This is the dynamic that we must follow. I wanted to play again, to be with the team. Especially being in Valladolid, where I had a great time and left many friends. We came out switched on and got a goal very early and once we went in front it was hard to beat us. We have to be self-critical. We could not give anything away. To win here we had to work and fight.

With Costa still suspended from European competition, Simeone watched his team salvage some pride from their trip to Moscow to face Rubin in the second leg of their Europa League tie at the Luzhniki Stadium as Falcao's late goal at least saw the team eliminated with an away win. And for the second match in a row, Falcao would prove the match winner, when he expertly converted his spot-kick against Espanyol at the Calderón following Héctor Moreno's poor challenge on Costa in the box to maintain the Rojiblancos' four-point gap over Real.

Three days later, Atlético travelled south to Andalusia

to face Sevilla in the crucial second leg of the Copa del Rey looking to at least protect the 2–1 lead they had earned at the Calderón a month before. With Falcao and Costa having struck up an impressive partnership, Simeone's two forwards aimed to fire Atlético into the final and a possible meeting with either Mourinho's Real or league leaders Barcelona.

With just six minutes played, Atlético drew first blood. Costa, collecting the ball on the edge of the box, twisted and turned before firing his shot past the outstretched hand of Beto in the Sevilla goal – his seventh goal in as many matches in the cup – to the delight of the travelling support. And on the half-hour mark, the deadly duo combined again to devastating effect to put the visitors firmly in the driving seat. When Costa picked up Falcao's pass on the left, he drove to the byline before crossing to the near post for '*El Tigre*' to fire Los Indios into a two-goal lead. The aggregate score was now 4–1 to Atlético, and with Simeone's men having notched two away goals already, it left Sevilla needing to score four of their own.

Seville-born winger Jesús Navas got one back before half-time to give the home support some prospect of a comeback but all hopes disappeared when Chilean hard man Gary Medel saw yellow for a blatant barge on Costa, before his angry protestations to the referee saw him dismissed immediately. Both teams missed gilt-edged chances to add to the scoreline before Croatian midfield maestro Ivan Rakitić fired home from 20 yards to restore parity on the night. However, the home side's frustration at their elimination at the final hurdle once again became apparent when young French midfielder Geoffrey Kondogbia saw red for a dangerous tackle from behind on Costa before standing on Atleti's number 19 to earn himself an early shower. After qualifying for the final and a showdown at the Bernabéu with Real, who had knocked Barcelona out 4–2 on aggregate in the other semi-final, Costa expressed his delight at the team's desire to go all the way:

> The team is good and that's why things are going well for me. I don't see myself as a figure, I keep working every day to improve. Hopefully we can go on like this. The aim of Atlético since I played the first match of the competition in Jaen was to get as far as possible and we are just one game away from lifting the title. This game is now a few months away so the focus will again return to the league. We wanted to get to the final but did not think about the opponent. Now we have to think about the league and continue our dynamic.

Real defeated Barca in Madrid for the second time in four days the following weekend, when a late goal from Sergio Ramos wrapped up a 2–1 *El Clásico* triumph to narrow the gap to second-placed Atlético to a solitary point. And with their city rivals breathing down their necks, Simeone's men dropped a further two points on the road when high-flying Málaga tightened their grip on the fourth Champions League spot with a hard-fought 0–0 draw on the Costa del Sol. And after a demoralising 1–0 home defeat at the hands of Real Sociedad where Atlético spurned chances galore and Costa was lucky to avoid another red card for what looked like an ugly stamp on substitute Imanol Agirretxe, Real's away win over Celta Vigo saw them leapfrog their rivals for the first time all season and into second place in La Liga.

On the back of his good form and blossoming partnership with Falcao, Costa celebrated a first call-up to the full Brazil squad ahead of the match with Sociedad at the Calderón. Upon receiving his maiden call from *Seleção* supremo Luiz Felipe Scolari, Costa told the Atlético club website:

It's the best thing that could happen in my career. It is a dream and the truth is I'm very happy. I think it was for the season we are having. It all depends on how things go. But it's much more for the team, which is good and in a final that counts a lot. He called to ask if I would play with the national team and I said it was a dream for me. He said he would call me one day and he was following me. It was a surprise.

Addressing Atlético's progress to the final of the Copa del Rey and the way his career had moved on from being shunted out on loan to all and sundry before and after his injury, Costa revealed his delight with the way things were now panning out for him:

The most important thing is to be in the final and to have our fans there. We're not bothered about playing there. When I got injured I was clear that I had to come back better. It would be very complicated but I had hopes of doing well and the truth is that everything is going well. Now, we must seize the moment and hopefully we can continue this. The coach has a great importance for all of us. He has brought peace to the group. It is very important to approach matches well for us. I will not change because it is the way I fight every day and it's my job. If I am where I am it is because of the way I have to approach things. I'm an awkward player on the field. They know that I will fight for everything. In football there is contact and fight and I will not chance how I play for anything. The referees do their job. I am sure that I am not being targeted by the referees.

To celebrate his international call, Costa, in his hundredth game in the Rojiblanco shirt, scored both goals to inspire Atlético to a 2–0 win over Osasuna in Pamplona. Costa struck either side of half-time to seal the points for the visitors. His first came courtesy of a simple header after the keeper had done well to save his initial effort, and three minutes after half-time he bundled home from close range to seal the points for Atlético. After the match the tough striker told the Atlético website: 'We have done well. I was lucky enough to score two goals in a very good match. It was a tough game. The victory says a lot about us. We deserve it and we are very happy.'

Having been called up to the national side by Scolari for the international friendlies with Italy and Russia, Costa returned to Madrid disappointed to have only played a total of thirty-four minutes from the substitutes' bench. Back in domestic action and with Real Madrid building up a head of steam in the race for runners-up spot in the table, Atlético dropped another two points with a 1–1 draw at home to Valencia and followed it up with an exasperating goalless draw on the road at Getafe where frustrations boiled over and Atlético's Mario Suárez and Diego Godín both saw red.

The team put the two draws behind them to keep up their

league challenge with a dominant 5–0 victory over Granada in front of their own fans in their next fixture. Costa opened the scoring with a brave header from Koke's floated cross, before the Brazilian, now a mainstay of Simeone's team, fed Falcao from the right wing to make it two. Falcao scored his second after the break before goals from Raúl García and the marauding Filipe Luís wrapped up a one-sided victory for the hosts. A solitary strike from Falcao at the Ramón Sánchez Pizjuán gave Atlético another win, their third in four games against Sevilla for the season, in a match which saw Costa pick up his fifth yellow card to leave him facing a ban and expulsion from playing in the Madrid derby the following week. However, after the yellow card was rescinded by the authorities, leaving Costa free to play, the newly capped Brazil striker took to the field alongside Falcao as Simeone sought to bring an end to Atlético's twenty-three-match winless streak against their eternal rivals from across the city.

Atlético went into the match at the Vicente Calderón knowing a victory would claw them back level with their rivals for second place. And as had happened so often in the past, Atlético came flying out of the blocks to take the lead, Falcao heading home Godín's cross after just four minutes to send the majority of the 53,000 crowd wild. However, Real, as they so often have done, struck back almost immediately – in fact, Juanfran turned the ball into his own net from Ángel Di María's dangerous free-kick. And the Argentine himself would prove the match winner in the second half, when latching onto Karim Benzema's defence-splitting pass he slid the ball past the helpless Courtois to extend their unbeaten run to twenty-four matches against Atlético.

The defeat, during which Costa picked up yet another yellow card to face a one-match suspension, meant Los Blancos extended their lead in second place over their city rivals to six points, but still a huge eleven points behind leaders Barcelona who now only required six points from their five remaining matches to clinch yet another La Liga title. In Costa's enforced absence, Atlético picked up a point on their travels away at Deportivo La Coruña and when he returned to the starting line-up against Celta Vigo four days later, the new Brazil international inspired his team to the three points required to secure Simeóne's pre-campaign target of Champions League qualification, with three games still to play.

Costa opened the scoring in Galicia just after half-time when he reacted quickest to Miranda's flick-on from a corner to head home from close range. Right back Juanfran added a second when he fired home from the edge of the area after Costa had invited him to shoot. Atleti were on their way back to the Champions League and despite Celta pulling one back late on, Simeone's men clinched the win with four minutes remaining when Falcao fired home high into the net. After the match, a delighted Costa told the press gathering:

The important thing was to win the match and secure the third place as soon possible. We now have some nice games coming up. We have a nice match against Barcelona on Sunday before the final. We cannot ask for anything more from the fans, they have been with us till the death all season, always encouraging. We must continue as we are and we really appreciate it. Hopefully we can enjoy so much more together. I'm working to improve every day. And for a team like Atlético you have to fight every day to play as there's a lot of competition out there. Hopefully that can help us continue to grow at Atleti.

Ahead of the Copa del Rey final in midweek, Atlético, able to relax after achieving their goal of qualifying for Europe's premier club competition, looked like upsetting champions Barcelona in front of a packed Vicente Calderón when Falcao fired them ahead in the fifty-first minute. However, twenty minutes from time Alexis Sánchez drew the Catalans level and an unfortunate own goal from captain Gabi saw Barca leave Madrid with the points. It was another disappointing result against one of Spain's big two clubs, but the real business would take place against Real in midweek at the Bernabéu.

30 October 1999: the last time Atlético had emerged victorious from a Madrid derby. Back then Claudio Ranieri was in charge of Los Colchoneros, and John Toshack of Real; and two goals from Atleti's Jimmy Floyd Hasselbaink and one from José Mari cancelled out Fernando Morientes' opener in front of 75,000 fans at the Bernabéu. It was a joyous day on the red and white side of the city divide. However, their joy was to be short-lived. At the end of that season Atlético were relegated from La Liga for the first time since before the Second World War, way back in 1933–4.

17 May 2013. It had been too long. It was time for Atlético to write some fresh history into the record books. The venue would be the Bernabéu, only this time it was the cup final. One final opportunity for Atlético to exorcise the ghosts and anguish of the past fourteen years, and it was at

the home of their greatest rivals. Being a final, and thanks to competition rules regarding allocation rights, Atlético would have at least 30,000 of their own fans to cheer them on inside the stadium. Atlético came into the match having secured Champions League football against Celta Vigo nine days earlier. Real, under Mourinho, had relinquished their league title to Barcelona and had been eliminated from the Champions League unexpectedly by German champions Borussia Dortmund at the semi-final stage. This was the last opportunity for both teams to claim silverware for the season, and with rumours circulating of Mourinho's likely return to Chelsea, it would be his final chance to sign off from the Bernabéu with a piece of silverware.

Things weren't harmonious in the Real camp, however. Mourinho had reportedly alienated himself from the media, the fans and even some of his squad having publicly criticised and dropped Pepe ahead of the final. Raúl Albiol started the match in the centre of defence alongside Sergio Ramos in Pepe's absence squaring up against Falcao, scorer of twenty-eight league goals, and Costa, top scorer in the tournament alongside Ronaldo with seven goals apiece. Speaking ahead of the historic kick-off to the Atlético website, Costa spoke of the team's desire to finally bring the team and the fans' long wait for a win over their rivals – in the most apt of settings – to a glorious end:

A final is always special, whoever it's against. There are many players who spend all year playing and not many have the opportunity to play a final. I think it's a unique moment. It is clear that people do not like this situation

[Atlético's twenty-four matches without a win over Real] but I think it does not affect us. We know it's a final and we have to do our best to win this game. The key to this final will be togetherness, to be a great team and for everyone to give their best. They have their stars and we have ours. Both teams have great players. Having Falcao is tremendous because if he's in the area he can score goals. No matter who scores, me, Falcao or Courtois, the important thing is to win the title.

Atlético were looking to make it four wins from five finals against their fierce rivals, the last having come back in 1992, while Real, conquerors of Atlético only once in a Copa del Rey final back in 1975, were looking to extend their unbeaten run against the Rojiblancos to twenty-five matches. And fourteen minutes into the match following a cagey opening, it was Real who made the breakthrough, Ronaldo escaping the attentions of Diego Godín from a Mesut Özil corner to head Los Blancos ahead. Following the goal, Atlético toiled while Real dominated possession. But with thirty-five minutes on the clock, parity was restored. After Mario Suárez dispossessed Ronaldo in midfield, Falcao came away with the ball, shrugging off the attentions of Albiol before sliding an inch-perfect pass into the path of Costa. And the Brazilian, by now the owner of a burgeoning reputation, motored away from Michael Essien and Fábio Coentrão to fire home a superb shot low and hard into the back of Diego López's net. It was game on.

Real came close to retaking the lead before the half-time whistle through Luka Modrić before Özil's low effort rebounded off a post as the game remained in the balance going into the break. After the restart, Filipe Luís looked on as his volley flew just wide before the woodwork once again came to the rescue of Thibaut Courtois' goal when Karim Benzema's shot had the big Atlético keeper beaten. And soon after, Atlético's woodwork was rattling once again when Ronaldo's smart free-kick under the Atlético wall failed to put Mourinho's men back in front. Atlético's goal was living a charmed life and with the match reaching fever pitch with tackles flying in left, right and centre and the referee's notebook beginning to fill up, Mourinho, visibly frustrated and prowling the touchline, suddenly snapped and lost his temper following an innocuous altercation between Suárez and Benzema.

To the delight of the Rojiblancos' supporters inside the Bernabéu, the referee sent Mourinho to the stands, in what would be his last game in charge of Real. With Mourinho down in the bowels of the Bernabéu and with the game petering out, thirty minutes of extra time awaited. Costa missed a glorious opportunity to put Atleti ahead for the first time in the tie, twice being denied by López in the Real goal. The breakthrough finally arrived when Miranda darted across the six-yard area to meet Koke's near-post corner kick to head home. Substitute Gonzalo Higuaín brought the best out of Courtois before the Belgian brilliantly denied Özil once again from point blank range. And with the game edging away from Los Blancos and the Atleti faithful airing a gleeful chant of 'Mourinho stay', tensions again boiled over when Ronaldo earned himself a red card for kicking out at Gabi, before the Atlético skipper received his own marching orders for encroaching at a free-kick to earn a second yellow card.

Atlético saw out the remaining seconds, however, and for

*Above left*: Diego Costa challenges Porto's Paolo Assunção during a Portuguese Premier League game between Braga and Porto, 3 March 2007. Porto won 1–0.

*Above right*: Not quite four years later, and the shirt – and team – have changed. Costa in the colours of Atlético Madrid during a Copa del Rey match against RCD Espanyol in Barcelona, 6 January 2011. The game ended in a 1–1 draw.

*Below*: Costa (right), then playing in Valladolid's midfield, celebrates with defender Javier Baraja after scoring against Sevilla during their Spanish League game at Jose Zorilla stadium in Valladolid on 13 April 2010.

*Above*: Copa del Rey final between Atlético and Real Madrid at the Bernabeu stadium, Madrid, 17 May 2013. Costa celebrates with teammates Arda Turan (centre) and Filipe Luis after scoring; Atlético won 2–1.

*Right*: Diego Costa in action for his native Brazil during the International Friendly match between Russia and Brazil at Stamford Bridge on 25 March 2013 – another 1–1 draw.

*Above*: Mourinho take note: Costa celebrates with teammates after scoring a penalty in Atlético's 3–1 win over Chelsea in their Champions League semi-final second-leg match at Stamford Bridge, 30 April 2014. Less than three months later the Brazilian had moved to Chelsea.
© Jean Catuffe/Getty Images

*Below left*: Not always cause for celebration: Costa leaves the field injured during the Champions League final between Atlético and Real Madrid in Lisbon, 24 May 2014. Real ran out 4–1 winners.
© Chris Brunskill Ltd/Getty Images

*Below right*: Time to celebrate again: Costa after scoring the opening goal in the Premier League game between Chelsea and Leicester City at Stamford Bridge, 23 August 2014. Chelsea won 2–0.
© Ian Kington/AFP/Getty Images

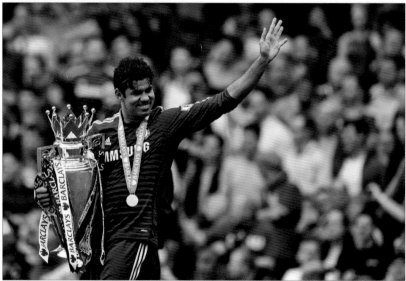

*Above*: Sidelined by injury from Chelsea's Premiership campaign, Costa watches from the stands with his brother Jair as his team take on Liverpool at Stamford Bridge on 10 May 2015. The game ended in a 1–1 draw, but by then nothing could stop Chelsea's march to the Premiership title. *Alex James/JMP/TEX Shutterstock*

*Below*: 'The Beast' with the Premiership trophy after Chelsea's win over Sunderland on 24 May 2015, the culmination of a brilliant campaign by Mourinho and his team in which Costa scored twenty goals.

© *Reuters/Dylan Martinez Livepic/Action Images*

the first time in fourteen years and twenty-five attempts they had defeated their nemesis, Real Madrid. The joy of their fans inside the stadium was immeasurable. The team had finally achieved what so many of their peers had failed to do: they had beaten Real Madrid, and in the Bernabéu. And in the final of the cup. The team and the fans would enjoy their moment inside their great rivals' cathedral of football as Gabi lifted the gigantic trophy aloft. Following all the post-match celebrations and laps of honour on the turf, Atlético coach Simeone, delighted at his team's gutsy performance, saluted his history-makers: 'We had the good fortune that a champion needs. What these players have done for the past year and a half is amazing. I don't have words for it.'

Meanwhile, Gabi, having lifted the trophy on behalf of the team for the tenth time in the club's 110-year history, told UEFA.com: 'This win is for all of those fans who were waiting fourteen years for us to beat Real Madrid. The team worked really hard ahead of this match, we worked to be here now standing on front of our fans.'

Following on from their historic win at the home of their great rivals, Atlético came back down to earth nine days later with an uninspiring 0–0 draw with Mallorca at the Calderón, although Simeone's men would finish the campaign on a high note when Costa scored twice in the dying moments to take a 3–1 win for Atlético in their final match of the campaign away at Zaragoza.

For Atlético it had been a wonderful season. Simeone had guided the club to their highest finish in the league since winning the title back in 1996. The team had ended their woeful run against Real, winning the Copa del Rey in the process for the first time in seventeen years. And for Costa, after scoring twenty goals in all competitions and forging a lethal partnership with Falcao, the campaign had been the most fruitful of his career to date. He had earned his third medal as an Atlético player. But this time, unlike the previous two occasions during which he had been an unused substitute, he had contributed massively on the field to help his team taste success. And for the first time in his career, the decision as to where he would be playing his football the following season would be completely in his own hands.

# CHAPTER 8

# EL CHOLO
# ('THE BEAST')

*'A lot of football success is in the mind. You must believe
you are the best and then make sure that you are.'*
Legendary former Liverpool manager Bill Shankly
explaining his formula for becoming the best

After completing his first full season back at the Vicente Calderón as a Copa del Rey winner, Costa, with twenty goals in forty-four appearances, had finally established himself as a key player in the Atlético Madrid squad. It had taken him over six years and numerous spells out on loan around Spain's lesser clubs to get there, and having finally gained the trust of the club's hierarchy he wasn't going to give it up without a fight. However, as is the norm in Spain, the majority of footballers have a contract which contains a release clause allowing interested parties to bypass the player's club and negotiate a move directly with the player. Costa's current contract contained such a clause.

The minimum release fee required to buy him out of his contract was rumoured to be £21 million. To the club this was fine as long as nobody activated the clause. However, in early August, the news broke that Liverpool Football Club had made a bid for the striker. The bid was believed to have been sufficient to activate Costa's release clause. With Luis Suárez attempting to force a transfer away from Anfield to Arsenal, it was believed the Reds were in the market for a replacement and had identified Costa as their preferred target.

Atlético had already lost Radamel Falcao at the end of May to ambitious Monaco, who also parted company with £60 million to purchase FC Porto pair João Moutinho and James Rodríguez. The club's prolific Colombian hitman departed the Vicente Calderón after two seasons and seventy goals for a mammoth £50 million fee. Simeone had already delved into the transfer market after Falcao's early summer departure to snap up Spain's record goalscorer David '*El Guaje*' Villa from Barcelona, and if the rumours circulating were to be believed he wouldn't stand in Costa's way if the big striker wanted to head to Merseyside and the English Premier League.

But Costa, after working so tirelessly to prove himself worthy of playing for a club of Atlético's stature, felt settled in Madrid and at peace and he had no intention of moving on at that moment. Having made his decision to turn down Brendan Rodgers' offer to join Liverpool, Costa explained his reasoning to Barcelona-based Spanish newspaper *Mundo Deportivo*:

> I was close to leaving Atlético. Liverpool are a great team, but after fighting so hard and overcoming difficulties to get my place at Atlético, how could I leave? I thought it was very important to keep growing with Atlético and to play there for many years.

## EL CHOLO ('THE BEAST')

It was a disappointment for the Kop faithful, although their disappointment would be softened by the news that Suárez's precocious talents would remain in Merseyside for a further season. But for the Rojiblancos, to hear Costa was staying after they had already lost Falcao, it was unreserved joy. Having committed his immediate future to Simeone's burgeoning project in addition to gaining dual citizenship at the beginning of July, thus freeing up a non-EU space within the squad, Costa put pen to paper on a new contract just ahead of the new season which tied him to the club until June 2018. The contract, whilst rumoured to have doubled his salary, also included a new buy-out clause that would stand at an increased £32 million. Speaking to Atlético's official website after confirming his desire to remain with the club after so many years of constant upheaval, a delighted Costa thanked the club for putting their trust in him:

> I am delighted with this agreement after fighting a long time to win the respect and affection of the fans, my team-mates and people in the club. It's a very special moment, I am very happy here. I thank the club for making me this offer to spend much more time here and hope to become a much bigger player and conquer all the objectives that the squad has.

Atlético Madrid sporting director José Luis Caminero confirmed the club's delight at securing Costa's services for the next five years, saying:

## DIEGO COSTA: 'THE BEAST'

This is great news for everyone at Atlético. This was one of the priorities of the club and it is great news for everyone at Atlético. Diego Costa is one of the key pieces of the squad and following our policy of keeping together the block that has given us so much success in recent years, extending his contract was one of our goals.

After missing out on a place in Luiz Felipe Scolari's squad for the summer's successful Confederations Cup campaign back in his homeland of Brazil despite making his international debut for the *Seleção* earlier in the year, Costa had returned to Madrid refreshed after his summer holidays looking forward to firing Atlético to further success. Speaking at a press conference after a training session at Atlético's Majadahonda Sports City training complex, Costa reiterated to the reporters present his delight at signing his new contract whilst also revealing his excitement ahead of the new season and the opening fixture away at Sevilla:

It was what I wanted, I am very happy to continue longer here and continue giving joy. After spending so much time fighting to have my place here, having won over the fans and everything, I never thought of leaving Atlético. I always need the pressure to feel good and to be motivated. I'll try to do better than last year, not only me but the whole group. The most important thing is that we all improve to succeed. The competition this year is very good. There is not much to say about David Villa, we all know what he can do. The other day he scored a goal on his debut [a friendly win over UD Las Palmas], which is very important to gain trust from the beginning. It is a good game to start the season. We know it is very important that we win the game and we know that they are a great opponent, but we are working hard to win not only this match but the following, we must go step by step. The Supercopa is a fruit of our hard work last year, but to do well first we have to win in Sevilla.

Down in the Andalusian capital, Costa set about celebrating his new deal in style. After Sevilla came within inches of opening the scoring when centre forward Carlos Bacca's diving header cannoned back off the bar, just thirty-five minutes into the new season Costa was up and running in the goalscoring stakes. Partnering debutant Villa in attack, Costa notched his first goal of the new campaign at the intimidating Ramón Sánchez Pizjuán when he latched onto Miranda's flick on from a corner to acrobatically volley the ball into the net. It was a fantastic start to the new season for Costa, but just two minutes later, Sevilla drew level when Diego Perotti smashed home a swerving shot superbly from 25 yards.

Despite Costa looking dangerous all evening, it was actually the hosts Sevilla who looked the more likely to take the lead with Atlético's Thibaut Courtois proving the busier of the two goalkeepers. However, with eleven minutes left on the clock, Costa latched onto a through ball from midfield artist Koke to slide the ball with unerring accuracy under the onrushing Beto to put Atlético in charge with the game heading towards its conclusion. And in injury time, substitute Cristian Rodríguez ran half the length of the pitch to wrap up the points with a wonderful solo goal as Atlético and Costa kicked off their season in style ahead of the Supercopa de España first leg with Barcelona at the Vicente Calderón three days later.

In front of a full house in Madrid, new signing Villa got his new club off to the perfect start against the reigning La Liga champions when he volleyed home magnificently from the edge of the area to put Atlético ahead with just twelve minutes played. Villa, having been discarded by the Blaugrana in the summer, celebrated wildly after putting his new club into the lead, dispelling the current common trend of not celebrating against former clubs. However, with Lionel Messi having been substituted at half-time by new Barca coach Gerardo Martino, it was another new signing, this time Neymar, who drew the visitors level with a far post header to leave the tie finely balanced ahead of the return leg at the Camp Nou the following week.

Four days later, Atlético welcomed Costa's former club Rayo Vallecano to the Calderón for the first home league match and the first derby of the new campaign. Having finished in the top half of the table at the end of the last campaign following their last second reprieval during Costa's last match for the club in 2012, Rayo came across the city looking to cause an upset. But from the outset it was obvious that a shock was not on the cards as a header from Raúl García, a close-range tap in from Costa, and a slick finish from Arda Turan courtesy of a classy assist from Costa, put Atlético three goals to the good by half-time.

Costa had spurned a great opportunity to fire Atleti into a four-goal lead before the break, but Simeone's men added further goals in the second forty-five courtesy of Tiago and a second at the death from Raúl García. The team travelled to Catalonia to face Barca in the second leg of the Supercopa de España in midweek in confident mood but returned empty-handed to the capital after failing to penetrate Víctor Valdés' goal, Barcelona sealing a record eleventh triumph in the process on away goals following the 0–0 draw at the Camp Nou.

However, Atlético's disappointment proved short-lived as goals from Villa and Koke inspired the team to a 2–1 league victory over Real Sociedad in San Sebastián. And following an international break that once again saw Costa completely ignored by Scolari for Brazil's friendly matches with Australia and Portugal, Atlético returned to league action with a thumping 4–2 victory over newly promoted Almería. Villa opened the scoring with his first league goal for the club at the Calderón, before Costa, showing the high level of confidence he was currently enjoying, saw his overhead kick from the edge of the box tipped over by the visiting goalkeeper.

After nearly executing a wonderful solo goal where the keeper once again denied him after the forward had scared his marker to death en route to goal, Costa finally got his goal from the penalty spot after Filipe Luís had been felled. Almería pulled one back but further goals from Tiago and Raúl García wrapped up a comfortable 4–2 win, their third in succession, to see them sharing a four-way lead of La Liga with Barca, Real and another newly promoted team, Villarreal.

Serving the third match of his four-match ban for head-butting Viktoria Plzeň defender David Limberský the previous season, Costa sat out the comfortable 3–1 victory over Zenit Saint Petersburg as Atlético got their Champions League campaign off to the best possible start. And to make up for his absence from European competition, he set about ensuring Atlético kept pace with the leaders at the top of La Liga with a 2–0 victory over another of his former employers, Real Valladolid, at the Estadio Nuevo José Zorrilla. Raúl García set Atlético on their way to a fourth straight league victory with a tremendous looping header, before Costa sped away from the static Blanquivioletas defence to slide home and wrap up an easy 2–0 victory at his former home.

Three days later, Costa, looking every inch a £32 million player, continued his fantastic start to the new campaign with two goals in front of the Rojiblanco faithful to inspire Atlético to three points against Osasuna. And four days after his cool finish and precise header gave Atleti a 2–1 win over the team from Pamplona, Costa was at it again when Simeone's men crossed the banks of the Manzanares River to face new head coach Carlo Ancelotti's Real in the Madrid derby.

Having finally broken their hoodoo against their great rivals in the cup final at the end of last campaign, surely Atlético couldn't repeat the trick. But with Falcao now history and Costa taking up the mantle of chief goalscorer, it was Atlético who broke the deadlock through that man Costa when he sprung the offside trap with a clever run off Álvaro Arbeloa's shoulder to slide his shot past onrushing Real goalkeeper Diego López. It was sweet retribution for Costa, who punished Real and their fans who had been singing 'Costa is not Spanish' in response to the rumours that he was considering switching allegiances to represent the Spanish national team.

With Real threatening a riposte of their own, Costa appealed in vain for a free-kick when Arbeloa appeared to barge him over before accidently catching him on the leg in the tangle that ensued, creating a large gash on the big man's shin. The right back would surely have been off if the referee had blown for a foul. In a game of cat and mouse, Pepe's remonstrations to the referee in the corner of the pitch for a seemingly innocuous hand-off from Costa fell on deaf ears. And before the break, finding space in the six yard area, Costa saw López bravely push away his shot on goal as tensions began to rise further with López and Costa going face-to-face and trading insults.

With Atlético still a goal to the good at half-time, Ancelotti introduced world-record £85 million signing Gareth Bale into the action after the interval, but it was Costa who came closest to adding to his earlier strike, López once again denying the big man when clean through on goal. Bale and Cristiano Ronaldo both threatened Courtois' goal before Koke struck the bar for the visitors. And in a ferocious finale, Courtois once again came to the rescue for Atlético when he pushed away Ronaldo's goal-bound scissors kick, to keep the score at 1–0 and deny Real a point. After waiting fourteen years and twenty-five matches to beat their fierce rivals, Atlético had now beaten them twice in two attempts, with Costa scoring in both encounters.

After watching Atlético sneak a late win over FC Porto in the Champions League, the last match of his suspension, Costa was back in the goals in the next fixture at the Calderón as he continued to grow in confidence with every match. Despite seeing a penalty saved in the first half of Atleti's 2–1 win over Celta Vigo, Costa recovered his composure to fire his team ahead in the first half after being denied a number of other scoring opportunities by Celta's inspired goalkeeper Yoel. And after creating a wonderful chance for Villa to make it two, only to see the experienced striker somehow put his shot wide, Costa took the responsibility upon his own shoulders to power away from his marker and slip his shot under Yoel for 2–0, his tenth goal of the season from only eight matches. He was on fire. Celta pulled one back with twenty minutes remaining to make things interesting before Yoel denied Costa late on to prevent the prolific marksman scoring the second hat-trick of his professional career.

Following yet another match-winning performance, one which kept Atlético's 100 per cent record intact to keep pace with Barcelona at the top of La Liga, Costa illustrated his team-over-personal glory attitude when he admitted it mattered not to him who scored the goals, as long as the team continued to win, whilst also answering a question about possibly representing La Roja in the future, with Vicente del Bosque allegedly showing interest in him:

The important thing is that we won, not who scored the goal. I'm very happy. I hate to miss penalties. It is a good thing I had the opportunity to score two more goals. I have no target. You have to go step by step and hopefully I can score a lot of goals. I've played my whole career here even though I was born in Brazil. Spain has given me everything and if I have to play with the national team, I'm going to do it the right way.

After the latest break for international fixtures, Costa and his team-mates, following their unbeaten start to the season, came crashing back down to earth when Courtois haplessly put through his own net as Espanyol inflicted a first defeat on Atlético. The team didn't have long to dwell on their maiden defeat of the season, however, as a trip to the Austrian capital Vienna lay in wait and a much-anticipated and long-awaited Champions League debut for Costa after the completion of his four-match suspension. It wouldn't take La Liga's leading marksman long to get into the groove against Austria Vienna.

Raúl García opened the scoring with the simplest of finishes with eight minutes played before Costa, attacking from his favoured inside left position, tormented his marker before sliding the ball past the advancing keeper for 2–0. It had taken him just nineteen minutes to make his mark on Europe's biggest stage. And after fifty-three minutes he wrapped up the win with his second goal of the night, showing neat control to side foot his team into an unassailable 3–0 lead. After the final whistle, he admitted his joy at finally getting the opportunity to grace Europe's biggest club competition: 'I really wanted to play in the Champions League. It is a competition that every player wants to play in. I am very happy with my debut and very happy with the team's win.'

Following on from his highly impressive debut in the Champions League, Costa and his team-mates swept Real Betis aside with consummate ease in the next league match played at the Calderón. Los Indios got the ball rolling after barely a minute's play when youngster Óliver Torres fired them ahead before a brace for Villa, an eleventh of the season for Costa and a rare strike from captain Gabi, condemned struggling Betis to another week in the relegation zone, whilst getting Atleti's challenge at the top of the table back on track. The previous evening's *El Clásico* had seen Barcelona overcome

Real 2–1 at the Camp Nou, resulting in Ancelotti's men losing further ground on their two biggest rivals.

Four days later a penalty apiece for Costa and Villa gave Simeone's men another hard-fought win on the road with a 2–1 triumph over Granada in Andalusia, before the same combination of players sealed a 2–0 victory at home to Athletic Bilbao, 'El Guaje' volleying home the opener before Costa sealed the points with a precise toe-poked finish at the Calderón to maintain Atlético's early-season challenge at the top of the table.

Another date with the Champions League beckoned as Atleti welcomed Austria Vienna to Madrid with the Copa del Rey winners looking to seal their place in the knockout stages after just four games. And the team did just that, with a simple 4–0 victory over their Austrian counterparts. Miranda got the ball rolling with a simple close-range finish, before Raúl García headed home Costa's cross and Filipe Luís notched his first goal of the campaign. And with eight minutes remaining, Costa got in on the act, firing home his obligatory goal after some great build-up play from Atlético.

Travelling to Valencia to face high-flying Villarreal the following weekend, Costa took to the field for his hundredth appearance in the red and white shirt of Atlético. However, the man also known as the 'Panther of the Manzanares', who had recently enjoyed a first call-up to the Spanish national squad for the upcoming friendlies with Equatorial Guinea and South Africa, was unable to celebrate the milestone with a goal as Atlético returned home from El Madrigal with a point following a 1–1 stalemate. To make matters worse, Costa limped off with a thigh injury that would ultimately rule him out of making his debut for La Roja.

## EL CHOLO ('THE BEAST')

After being forced to withdraw from del Bosque's national team squad, Costa spent the time at Atlético's Majadahonda Sports City training complex receiving physiotherapy in an effort to be fit for the visit of Getafe to the Calderón. And after recovering sufficiently to take a place on the substitutes' bench, Costa, with the team cruising 4–0 thanks to an own goal, one from Villa and two from Raúl García, entered the action and within seven minutes got his name on the score sheet with a goal of the season contender. Latching onto Gabi's long cross from the right, Costa, showing no ill-effects from his injury, leapt in the air with his back to goal to fire a spectacular overhead kick into the top corner of the net to make it 5–0. A wonderful piece of artistry from Costa. Goals six and seven followed from Villa and another substitute, Adrián López, to wrap up a breathtaking victory and push Atlético back above neighbours Real into second place in the league table.

Mindful of not placing too much pressure on Costa's body, with him only just back from injury, Simeone and the squad made the long trip to Russia to take on Zenit in Saint Petersburg without their main man in tow for their latest Champions League match. Atlético returned home to Spain with a creditable 1–1 draw and the point required to finish as group winners. And after benefitting from a few extra days rest, Costa returned to Simeone's starting eleven for the trip to Elche near the Mediterranean coast. After a number of missed chances, Atlético finally took the lead just past the hour when Koke capitalised on some laboured defending to put the visitors one goal to the good. Ten minutes later Costa clinched another three points for Atleti to draw them equal with leaders Barcelona at the league summit when he sprinted clear of the home defence to side foot Adrián's delicious assist into the net. And with Barcelona succumbing to a 1–0 defeat at the hands of Athletic Bilbao in the Basque Country, Simeone and his squad were back level with their illustrious rivals from Catalonia on forty points from fifteen matches.

Atlético powered past minnows UE Sant Andreu 4–0 as they began their defence of the Copa del Rey in menacing fashion, before the team finished the group phase of the Champions League with a fifth win from six matches as they beat FC Porto 2–0 at the Calderón. Raúl García opened the scoring early in the first half with a wonder goal from the tightest of angles. Costa wrapped up a composed win before half-time when he sprung the offside trap to calmly round Helton in the visitors' goal before slotting the ball home from another relatively tight angle. It proved a great way for Costa to celebrate his candidacy for the FIFA/FIFPro World XI nominations for best strikers in recognition of his outstanding form over the past year for the Rojiblancos.

Match day seventeen saw Atlético finish the first part of the season still equal with leaders Barcelona on forty-six points after defeating Levante 3–2 thanks to a late winner from the irrepressible Costa at the Vicente Calderón. Levante had shocked the home crowd in the opening seconds as Andreas Ivanschitz strode through to beat Courtois with barely a minute played. But the home team bounced back after twenty-nine minutes when Diego Godín, so dangerous from set pieces, climbed highest from a corner to power home his header.

And with two minutes of the second half played, Costa appeared unmarked at the back post as he crashed his left-footed volley into the net and put Atlético in charge. But within ten minutes Levante had shocked the hosts once again when

## EL CHOLO ('THE BEAST')

Pedro Ríos streaked away to level the score. However, with only fourteen minutes left and the match heading towards a draw, right back Juanfran ghosted in undetected at the back post and when he was felled, Costa stepped up to calmly dispatch his penalty and win the game for Los Colchoneros. Speaking after Levante had given them one of their toughest tests of the season to date, Costa stressed in the post-match press conference that the key to maintaining their good form was teamwork over individual glory:

> It was an important game to finish the year winning, the team is in good shape, things are going well for me personally and I hope they keep it up. The most important thing is the team, a striker always needs goals, but what really matters is that these goals help to score points. The team must follow the same dynamics to go far. The players have suffered today. It has been very hard, but great teams have to know how to play these games.

Atlético were lying in second place going into the Christmas break. But could they really sustain a challenge to the might of Barcelona or Real Madrid and break their rivals' ten-year grip on the championship? Were they capable of winning a first La Liga title since 'El Cholo' lifted the trophy as team captain way back in 1996? With Costa banging in the goals, left, right and centre, nineteen in total before Christmas, there was a chance, albeit a small one, given the size and depth of Barcelona and Real's squads. But if Simeone could keep his men fit and hungry anything would be possible, perhaps even Champions League success.

# CHAPTER 9

# CAMPEONES!

*'Partido a partido.'*
Head Coach Diego Simeone explains the philosophy behind
Atlético's charge towards a first title in eighteen years:
'Match-by-match, one game at a time'

When the Atlético Madrid squad reported back for training following their Christmas break, they did so as joint leaders of La Liga. It would take one almighty effort from the squad if they were still to be challengers come the end of the season in mid-May. And although they toiled throughout their first match back after the New Year, midfielder Koke was in the right place at the right time on seventy minutes to give Atlético their first vital win of 2014 ahead of their return to Copa del Rey action away at Valencia in midweek.

And the team came within a matter of seconds of leaving the Mestalla with an impressive victory after Raúl García had headed them into the lead with twenty minutes remaining, only for Portuguese striker Hélder Postiga to grab a dramatic equaliser in the final minute for the hosts to set up an intriguing second leg the following week back in Madrid. Before that encounter though, there was the small matter of La Liga giants and table-toppers Barcelona coming to town. This would be the true test of Simeone and Atlético's championship credentials, even if at this stage of the season they were playing the whole 'contenders for the title' question down. However, if they could beat Barca at a packed and rocking Vicente Calderón, Simeone's men would well and truly be throwing down the gauntlet to the reigning league champions.

In a somewhat baffling team selection, Barca head coach Gerardo Martino opted to leave Lionel Messi and Neymar, his two main attacking threats, on the bench for the first forty-five minutes of the clash between La Liga's top two. And although both entered the fray at the interval, it was the hosts who enjoyed the clearer opportunities throughout the match, with Costa wasteful in front of goal. However, with both sets of players proving profligate the match ended in stalemate, a satisfactory result for both teams. Atlético got back to winning ways following two consecutive draws when Valencia visited the Calderón for the second leg of the Copa del Rey last sixteen. Gabi provided the assists for both goals as headers from Diego Godín and Raúl García ensured progression to the quarter-finals and a clash with Athletic Bilbao, winners of the competition twenty-three times (but not since 1984).

With Barcelona also progressing into the last eight of the cup, both Atlético and the Catalans dropped valuable points in their next league matches. Atlético allowed Sevilla to recover from a goal down to take a share of the spoils at the Calderón, while Barca also dropped two important points on the road against Levante allowing Real Madrid to edge their way back into the title mix. Atlético overcame Athletic Bilbao 1–0 at the Calderón thanks to a headed winner from Diego Godín to secure Simeone's men the advantage in the Copa del Rey quarter-final first leg. And following two draws and only two goals in three league matches, Atlético made the short journey across the city to face Costa's former club Rayo Vallecano at the Campo de Fútbol de Vallecas the following Sunday evening. Although he would create the opening goal for David Villa, Costa, still without a goal in 2014, would once again finish the match without seeing his name on the score sheet. But as he had stated on a number of occasions throughout the season already, it wasn't about how many goals he could score, it was about the team getting results. Further goals from Arda Turan and an own goal from Rayo gave Atleti a crucial 4–2 victory to keep pace with Barca who won 3–0 at home to Málaga.

Any concerns that Costa had lost his scoring touch were dispelled in the very next game as the team recovered from a goal down to progress to the semi-finals of the Copa del Rey at the expense of Bilbao, thanks to a well-taken volley from Raúl García and a late clincher from Atlético's top goalscorer. And Costa also found his scoring boots in the league in the very next game as the club and the stadium as a whole paid a moving tribute before kick-off to legendary former Atlético Madrid centre forward and manager Luis Aragonés who had passed away at the age of seventy-five from leukaemia the previous day. Aragonés, to this day Atlético's record goalscorer, had also managed the club on four separate occasions and set the wheels in motion for La Roja's global domination when he guided Spain to a 1–0 victory over Germany in the final of the European Championship in 2008, thanks to a goal from another Atlético great, Fernando Torres.

## DIEGO COSTA: 'THE BEAST'

Real Sociedad were the visitors to the Vicente Calderón on an emotional evening as Atlético looked to pay a fitting homage to Aragonés with the victory that would see them go three points clear at the top of the table following Barcelona's surprising 3–2 home defeat the previous evening at the hands of Valencia. And following all the heartfelt pre-match tributes and with the club's flag flying at half-mast over at the training ground, it was Costa who provided the ball for Villa to fire home and spark mass celebrations around the ground. Raising his hands to the sky in tribute to his former mentor with Spain, Villa had set Atlético on their way to the summit. The Rojiblancos would have to wait until the seventy-second minute for the clinching goal when Costa strode through unopposed to make it 2–0, his first goal since returning to the club in January, before further goals from Miranda and Diego Ribas added gloss to the scoreline to leave Atlético perched at the top of La Liga on a poignant evening that Aragonés would have thoroughly appreciated.

Simeone's charges were, however, humbled 3–0 in the first leg of their Copa del Rey semi-final as Real Madrid brought Atleti back down to earth with a bump and exacted revenge for their defeat in last season's final and at the Bernabéu earlier in the season. Pepe silenced the small number of visiting supporters when his deflected shot deceived Courtois to fly into the net in the opening quarter, and after half-time Los Merengues piled on the misery for their city neighbours when Jesé Rodríguez slipped a deft shot under Courtois' body to make it 2–0. Costa, never backward in coming forward against Real, soon entered the referee's notebook. After being bundled over by Real winger Ángel Di María, the burly forward kicked out at the lightweight Argentine, luckily only receiving a yellow card and not a straight red. Pepe and Costa, never the best of friends, eyeballed one another.

Atlético's miserable evening was to get even worse on seventy-four minutes when another sizeable deflection saw Di María's long-range effort leave Courtois wrong-footed as Real took an ominous step towards the final ahead of the return fixture across the city the following week. Atlético's dismal result at the Bernabéu was followed by an even more shocking 2–0 reverse away at struggling Almería before their week from hell was topped off with another lacklustre 2–0 home defeat to Real in the return leg of the cup, two early Ronaldo penalties doing the damage to bring Atleti's defence of their crown to a dismal end.

The team bounced back from their mini run of bad form to put away two goals in the first four minutes at home to Real Valladolid, Raúl García pouncing first to finish sweetly from the edge of the area after a clever free kick from Gabi. And within sixty seconds, Costa latching onto a long through ball from Garcia lifted the ball over the advancing goalkeeper to make it two. Atleti were back in the groove and a second-half header from Godín, proving a useful set piece outlet once again, finished Valladolid off to ease Atlético's disappointment of the previous week's poor results. After their morale-boosting win ahead of the Champions League clash with seven-times champions AC Milan, Costa spoke to the press, explaining the run of poor form they had suffered was something to be expected during the course of a busy season:

The crisis was there, we knew this could happen. People doubt you after three defeats, but in the changing room we did not. We played two games in quick succession with a great team like Madrid, but after that, no doubt we go out to win and we did. Milan are a great team, with a great tradition, and can play these games. To take something we have to play a complete game and we will go with that mentality.

Milan came out at the San Siro looking determined and ready to take the game to Atlético with Kaká, the former Real Madrid attacker, spurning three glorious chances to put the Rossoneri into a first-half lead. And with the game still scoreless going into the last ten minutes it was Costa who popped up at the far post to head a poor defensive clearance into the net for the winning shot, a priceless away goal. Talking about how difficult the match had been against such experienced European royalty, Costa praised the togetherness of the Atlético squad and singled out his goalkeeper Courtois for special praise. The young Belgian international had come to Atleti's rescue on numerous occasions throughout the ninety minutes, and Costa commented:

They were a very difficult team and it was a big game, but we have known when to take the pressure at the key moment and get the result. The best feature we have had today is that we knew we could get a result and we have been very close together. In the end the victory is a great result. Courtois is one of the best goalkeepers in the world. He knows, he has power and has our confidence.

Courtois gives us a lot and always gives us amazing help. We know it is not over. We have a good result but Milan are a great team and anything can happen in the second leg. We have a great advantage and we will try to keep it at the Calderón.

After the impressive victory in Italy, Atlético returned to La Liga action looking to return home to the capital with all three points from the trip to Pamplona to face Osasuna. However, within forty-five minutes played and Simeone's men suffering a European hangover, the game was already over as Osasuna blasted out of the blocks at their El Sadar ground to lead 3–0 at half-time. It was Atleti's second league defeat since Christmas and another defeat against the teams in the league they needed to be beating in order to stay in with a chance of winning the championship. The defeat coupled together with Barcelona's surprising 3–1 loss the previous day to Real Sociedad and also Real Madrid's easy 3–0 victory over Elche, saw Carlo Ancelotti's men leapfrog Atlético and Barcelona into first position in the league for the first time during the season.

It wasn't in any way, shape or form good preparation for the Madrid derby to come, but after falling behind to Karim Benzema's early goal Atlético should have been awarded a penalty when Sergio Ramos brought Costa down in the area only for the referee to award a goal kick. Costa, who had just been included in the Spanish squad for the first time ahead of the friendly match with Italy at Atlético's Vicente Calderón stadium, was livid and let the referee know it. Before the break, Atleti turned the scoreline on its head, however, when first Koke smashed a brilliant goal past Diego López from an angle, before the skipper Gabi rifled home an unstoppable shot from fully 35 yards to put Los Indios in the lead. Costa missed a chance to stretch Atlético's lead after escaping Pepe's clutches in the second half and then watched his header sail agonisingly wide from Gabi's corner. Costa picked up his almost obligatory yellow card against Real in the second half, but after failing to punish Real with any further goals despite creating chance after chance, it was Ronaldo, inevitably, leading the race with Messi and Costa for the Pichichi, who fired home a late equaliser to maintain Los Blancos' position at the summit of La Liga.

With thirteen games of the Spanish league season remaining and Atlético lying two points behind their great rivals at the top of the table, two goals in three minutes from Villa secured the Rojiblancos a priceless win on the road against Celta in Vigo. Costa, having missed the victory in north-west Spain returned to the starting line-up for the visit of Milan to the Calderón for their Champions League second leg match, with Atlético holding the one-goal advantage they had earned the previous week in Lombardy. And Atlético's star attraction returned with a bang as the team overwhelmed Clarence Seedorf's in-decline outfit 4–1 on the night and 5–1 on aggregate, an ominous warning to the other seven teams left in the quarter-final draw.

Costa set Atlético on their way with just three minutes played, volleying Koke's pinpoint cross acrobatically into Christian Abbiati's net. The lead lasted just twenty-four minutes, however, as Kaká headed home a fantastic centre to give the Italians hope. But that hope was all but extinguished five minutes before the break, when Arda Turan picking up the ball on the edge of the Milan box, juggled it a little before volleying a looping shot into the top corner for 2–1. Raúl García headed home Atlético's third before Costa strolled through the Milan defence almost unopposed to rifle home his second of the night to wrap up a thumping victory and with it progress to the quarter-finals. Not bad progress considering it was Atlético's first season back in the Champions League for four years.

Costa, having relocated his scoring boots, should have been awarded a first-half penalty against Espanyol at the Calderón the following weekend, only for the referee to turn a blind eye once again. However, the man from Lagarto was not to be denied and he got his goal in the fifty-fifth minute after outmuscling his marker to latch onto Villa's through pass and side foot home the game's only goal. Costa notched again in Atleti's next match on the road at relegation-doomed Real Betis in Seville, his twenty-second of a magnificent season. In the first half, Costa had had a goal wrongly scrubbed for offside, but in the second half, after Betis were reduced to ten men, Gabi put Atlético on their way with another long-range special before Costa anticipated Koke's wonderful knock-down to fire Los Colchoneros to another three points.

And after Barcelona's thrilling 4–3 victory over Real at the Bernabéu in *El Clásico*, Simeone's team moved up into top spot for only the second time that season with nine matches left to play. Atlético maintained their one-point lead over Barcelona at the top of La Liga in midweek when Costa headed home from January loan-signing José Sosa's corner for the winner against Granada, before the team returned home to Madrid from the Basque Country with a priceless 2–1 victory over Athletic Bilbao to sustain their momentum. Iker Muniain opened the scoring for the hosts with a spectacular finish early on, but Costa hauled Atlético level fifteen minutes later, displaying tremendous pace to accelerate away from the Bilbao defence and deftly slide home the equaliser. And Costa was yet again denied a clear-cut penalty after being brought down in the second half, before Koke combined with Filipe Luís to head home the winner on fifty-five minutes.

Following four goals in consecutive games in March to help Atleti return to the top of the table, Costa was voted La Liga's player of the month for March. After nearly a month away from Champions League action, Atlético squared up to an all-Spanish quarter-final with Barcelona on 1 April at the Camp Nou, looking for a positive result to take back home to Madrid ahead of the second leg in eight days' time. Worryingly for Simeone, though, Costa limped off on the half-hour mark following a tussle with Sergio Busquets that left him nursing his right thigh. Nevertheless, the visitors recomposed themselves after the loss of their inspirational goal-getter to notch a priceless away goal when Diego Ribas, having re-joined the club in January to aid Atlético's push for honours, picked up possession from a quick free kick before smashing an unstoppable shot past José Manuel Pinto in the Barcelona goal to leave Simeone grinning on the touchline from ear to ear. A marvellous pass from Andres Iniesta, however, teed up Neymar to fire home an equaliser, but for Atlético a draw and an away goal in the Camp Nou was a great result. Now all they needed to do was get Costa back to fitness for the rest of the campaign to give them a realistic shot at winning a trophy or possibly even two.

With their main source of goals still side-lined by injury, it was Raúl García, who had chipped in with a number of important goals throughout the campaign, who put away the only goal of the game in Atleti's clash with Villarreal at the Calderón, another priceless three points with the games running out. And after Koke had fired home the only goal of the Champions League quarter-final second leg against Barca at the Camp Nou, Atlético were starting to contemplate the possibility of completing a previously unthinkable double.

Barcelona slipped to an untimely 1–0 defeat away at Granada following their Champions League elimination at the hands of Atlético, while Real Madrid continued to apply pressure to their cross-city rivals in the race for the title with another four-goal haul against Almería. Having recovered from his thigh injury, Costa gave the club a massive and timely boost when he returned to Simeone's starting eleven for the trip to Getafe and watched on as Godín once again climbed highest to head the visitors into a half-time lead.

Costa missed the chance to wrap up the points for the visitors just past the hour when Getafe's goalkeeper Jordi Codina got down to save his spot kick superbly. But the big man was not to be denied a comeback goal and he displayed courage beyond the call of duty when he slid in at the back post to turn the ball home from close-range. However, having only just returned from one injury it looked likely that Costa would be set for another spell in the treatment room, when having concentrated all his attention on putting the ball in the back of the net, he collided with the upright to leave his shin gushing with blood. After the match, Simeone allayed fears over his star striker's fitness, quipping: 'Another cut doesn't harm the tiger. Anyway, it's the post I feel sorry for.'

With the ultra-competitive Costa patched up and itching to get back in the action, Simeone obliged his top goalscorer by throwing him straight back into the team to face Elche five days later. Villa squandered a first-half penalty to settle the team's nerves and it took Atlético until the seventy-second minute to finally break the deadlock when Miranda headed home brilliantly from Sosa's corner. And in the dying seconds Costa stepped up to the penalty spot to confirm the points after he was felled with just the goalkeeper to beat, confirming Atlético's position at the top of the table with just four matches remaining.

José Mourinho's Chelsea arrived at the Calderón on 22 April looking to take a positive result back to England, but after a game of few chances, the two teams played out a scoreless draw to leave the door firmly ajar for both teams to win through to the Champions League final on 24 May in Lisbon. Nil-nil was a dangerous result for Chelsea. It effectively meant any away goals for Atlético would count as double. Sandwiched between the semi-final legs, a solitary Raúl García header won Atlético another three vital points against Valencia before the Rojiblancos travelled to west London to try and qualify for the Champions League final.

With confidence riding high in the Atleti camp ahead of the tie at Stamford Bridge with the club still top of La Liga, the match was set to be a real cracker, with Mourinho's men having just dealt Liverpool's Premier League title hopes a major blow with a 2–0 victory at Anfield. And it was the home side who struck the first blow, ex-Atlético idol Fernando 'El Niño' Torres sweeping the Blues into the lead after thirty-six minutes. However, Atlético forward Adrián López popped up unmarked ahead of a sleeping Chelsea defence to equalise just before half-time to give Atlético that vital away goal.

On the hour mark, Costa, performing an early audition for the role of Chelsea's next centre forward, drew a clumsy challenge from Samuel Eto'o who tripped him just inside the box to give Atlético a golden opportunity to leave Chelsea needing two goals to qualify for the final. The big man picked himself up off the floor, and despite the best efforts of the Chelsea fans behind the goal, drilled his penalty high into the net. Atlético had one foot in the final. And when Arda Turan tucked home a third with eighteen minutes remaining to leave Chelsea needing three goals, it was game over. A mouth-watering final in Lisbon against Carlo Ancelotti and his Galacticos, who themselves had cantered past Pep Guardiola's reigning European champions 5–0, was the reward.

Talking to the press after the final whistle, a delighted Costa revealed his joy at reaching the final whilst also praising the inspirational Simeone for getting them to the Lisbon showpiece: 'We've done everything to be in the final. We justly deserve to be in the final. The team was calm. Torres scored a goal but we knew a goal from us was worth double. The team has been amazing. The mister, as always in the key moments, has the definite word'.

However, with three matches of the Spanish league left for Atlético to secure a first title in eighteen years, all thoughts of Lisbon and the final would need to be put aside for the time being. With three teams still in the race, total concentration would be needed. Atlético's weekend began brilliantly when Madrid-based club Getafe did them a massive favour, grabbing a late equaliser to secure a 2–2 draw with Barcelona at the Camp Nou. However, misfortune struck for Atleti the very next day when Simeone watched his team crash to a 2–0 defeat away at Levante. Thankfully for Simeone and their supporters' blood pressure, on a crazy weekend in the title race, Valencia managed to take two points off Real at the Bernabéu, although things could have been even worse for Real if Ronaldo hadn't popped up with an injury-time equaliser.

Costa's former club Valladolid granted Atlético and their former striker a huge favour in midweek when they equalised late in their match at Estadio Nuevo José Zorrilla against Real Madrid. Sergio Ramos' first-half goal looked to have secured the points for the visitors only for La Pucela to equalise five minutes from time to keep their own faint hopes of avoiding the drop intact. And going into the penultimate weekend of the campaign where all the teams would kick off at the same time, there were only four points separating the top three. Atlético's destiny lay in their own hands.

Atlético were up against Málaga at the Calderón. But Simeone would have to do without Costa for the crucial match after his twenty-seven-goal striker damaged a muscle in training. Elsewhere, Ancelotti's Real would have to travel to Vigo to face Celta while Barcelona would head south expecting a straightforward victory in Valencia against struggling Elche. And in yet another tense storybook turn of events, Atlético, who could have secured the title with a win depending on results elsewhere, could only garner a 1–1 draw against Bernd Schuster's Málaga in front of their frustrated fans in Madrid.

However, amazing news came out of Elche's Estadio Manuel Martínez Valero in Valencia. Barcelona had been thwarted by a stubborn Elche side battling for their lives, only mustering a 0–0 draw. Meanwhile, even more amazingly, over in Vigo, two goals from Brazilian-born striker Charles had shocked Real Madrid, ruling them out of contention for a record thirty-third league title.

It all meant that with Real no longer in contention, Atlético would have to go to Catalonia and a capacity Camp Nou tasked with avoiding defeat to lift the La Liga title. It would need a 'Roy of the Rovers' moment it seemed for Atlético to deny their hosts the title. For Barcelona anything less than a win would not suffice. They had to win. In the build-up to the vital match, Costa's injury situation improved to such an extent that 'El Cholo' decided his fragile fitness was worth the risk and named his main man to start on Atlético's date with destiny.

And so to the big day, winner takes all. But with just fourteen minutes played, disaster struck for Costa and Atlético. Whilst striding forward in support of a dangerous attack, Atleti's main goalscoring threat pulled up with a reoccurrence of his thigh injury. His game was over. Atlético would have to do it without him. And soon after, they were dealt another huge blow when chief creator Arda Turan fell awkwardly on his back, leading to his own withdrawal in floods of tears. Things couldn't get any worse, surely. Well yes they could, as it happened. Just past the half-hour mark things looked decidedly bleak for Simeone and his men. Having lost their two main threats, Alexis Sánchez scored a wonder goal, his nineteenth of the season, to put Barca into the lead and send the Blaugrana faithful into ecstasy. Surely the title was Barca's now?

Into the second half, and it was David Villa, Barca's former striker, who was first to get a shot in as he watched his effort come back off a post. Maybe it wasn't Atleti's day. And a second effort saw Pinto stand firm to turn his shot away to safety. However, with only four minutes of the second half played and with Atlético applying heavy early second-half pressure, Diego Godín, as he had done on seven occasions already during this incredible campaign, rose highest to meet Gabi's dangerous corner. His bullet header flew into the corner of Pinto's net. Goal! 1–1. Incredible! The small pocket of away fans amongst the 97,000 capacity crowd went wild. The remainder fell silent for a moment. Simeone's men were back in the driving seat, masters of their own destiny once more.

With the clock ticking down, Martino introduced Neymar from the bench as the hosts desperately sought the goal that would win them and not Atlético the title, their twenty-third. And it looked as if Messi, kept quiet on the whole during the match, had done it when he put the ball into the net midway through the second half. As he wheeled away in delight to celebrate, however, he spied the assistant's flag. He had strayed offside. No goal. It remained all square. Courtois tipped over a speculative effort from Dani Alves and Gerard Piqué went down in the area, appearing to look for a penalty, but in the end it all proved in vain as the referee remained unmoved. Atlético held fast and when referee Antonio Mateu Lahoz blew his whistle for the final time in the match, it signalled the end of eighteen long years of pain for Los Colchoneros and their long-suffering supporters.

The joy on the faces of those Atleti supporters lucky enough to be in the stadium was clear for all to see. The players fell to their knees on the pitch as the realisation of their achievement sank in. Costa ran on to celebrate with his team-mates, seemingly oblivious to the pain of his injury. Simeone embraced his staff and applauded the Catalan crowd. And with typical grace, they applauded him back. Atlético had deserved it. Simeone and his team had made history. Part one of the double was complete. In one week's time, it would be time for part two. Before the Champions League final, the team, after arriving back in Madrid, embarked upon the traditional open-top bus tour.

Unfortunately, because La Liga chief Ángel María Villar was away, the bus parade took place without the famous La Liga trophy. However, for fans of Atlético, who had had to endure so many celebratory tours by their fierce rivals from across the river, it mattered not. The title, Atlético's tenth in total, was theirs. They could wait until the start of the next season to be presented with their trophy. The day belonged to the club and they intended to enjoy it with or without their prize.

After working all week in an effort to try and recover sufficiently to take the field against Real in Lisbon, Costa came through an hour's training the night before the season's showpiece final. And Simeone, having been convinced for the second time in a week of his star man's fitness, decided he would take the risk and hand Costa his number 19 jersey to start the final from the first whistle. However, after nine minutes, Simeone's calculated risk once again backfired. Costa pulled up whilst in full gallop and had to be withdrawn, to be replaced by Adrián.

Welshman Gareth Bale, in his first season as a *Madridista*, squandered a glorious first-half opening to put Real ahead, before that man Godín once again found himself in the right place at the right time to nod Atlético ahead following Iker Casillas' blunder. For the remaining fifty-four minutes of the match and injury time Atlético clung on to their lead heroically. But then with the game in its final embers, Ramos rose highest from a corner kick three minutes into injury time to head Real level. It was sheer devastation for Atlético.

A first Champions League crown had been snatched away from them at the death. Only once in their 111-year history had they made it to a European Cup final before, back in 1974. On that occasion in Belgium's now-infamous Heysel Stadium, after ninety goalless minutes the match against Franz Beckenbauer's Bayern Munich went into extra-time. And with just seven minutes remaining, Luis Aragonés fired home a wonderful curling free kick to put Atlético on the verge of European glory. However, with just one minute of extra time left to play, Bayern equalised and with no penalty shoot-outs to settle the European Cup final in those days, Atlético having expended all their energy already, lost the replay 4–0. History, it seemed, was about to repeat itself.

For Real, the dream of *La Decima* – the club's tenth European crown – was back on. Ancelotti's men had already won the Copa del Rey title vacated by Atlético with victory over Barcelona at the Mestalla in mid-April. And in the second half of extra time, Real, having gained the ascendancy with that Ramos header in the dying seconds of normal time, pounced three times in the extra thirty minutes through Bale, Marcelo and a Ronaldo penalty to finally claim *La Decima*, after a twelve-year wait. After the match Simeone admitted his risk in starting Costa had backfired: 'It was my mistake. It cost us.'

For Simeone, Costa and everybody associated with Atlético, there was disappointment in having recreated history and lost in such a manner to their greatest rivals, but in hindsight they will feel rightly proud of their achievements in 2013–14. It was a season where they made history, after all. No longer could the club be described as '*El Pupas*' or the jinxed one as it had been for so long. Atlético were finally back on top of the pile.

It was a team effort. But has one man ever taken a team to a different level in the way that Diego Costa did? Perhaps. Perhaps not? With his goals, fighting spirit and sheer will to win, having dragged Atlético to the La Liga title and to the brink of Champions League glory, one thing is for certain, supporters of Los Colchoneros will never forget him. And when he eventually retires back to his home in the north-east of Brazil as he has indicated he will do, Costa will probably look back and think to himself, 'That was one hell of a season when we [Atlético] upset the applecart to snatch the title from Barcelona and Real Madrid.' And he'd be right.

# CHAPTER 10

# TUG OF WAR

'He is turning his back on the dream of millions to represent
the five-time world champions at the World Cup in Brazil.'
Luiz Felipe Scolari reacts angrily to Costa's decision to switch
allegiances and represent Spain rather than the country of his birth

**B**razil has a long-standing reputation for producing some of
the greatest, most technically gifted and watchable
footballers that lovers of 'the beautiful game' have ever had
the pleasure of viewing. The country boasts legendary players,
coaches and teams that live on in the memories of all those
that have witnessed their greatness. Pelé, Garrincha, Tostão,
Jairzinho, Zico, Careca, Romário, Ronaldo, all legends of
Brazilian football's glorious past; all are heroes to a proud
nation of people who share three major passions in life:
religion, carnival and football.

The World Cup-winning teams of 1958, 1962 and 1970
still to this day evoke memories of the style of football that
Brazil is famed for embracing while the class of 1982 is widely
recognised as the greatest team in history not to have ended the

tournament holding aloft the eighteen-carat gold prize (fans of the 1974 'total-football' inspired Dutch and Johan Cruyff may disagree). However, not every Brazilian professional footballer enjoys the hero worship bestowed upon the greats of yesteryear. Indeed, some are looked upon with utter disdain. Some are regarded as un-Brazilian. One in particular set the flames of discontent ablaze in the summer of 2014 like none before. His identity? One Diego Costa.

12 June 2014. A historic date. The setting? The Arena de São Paulo in South America's largest city, São Paulo. For millions of Brazilians worldwide this was the day when their dreams of an eventual date with destiny would begin. The event? Brazil versus Croatia and the long-awaited start of the greatest show on earth – the 2014 football World Cup. And not just any old World Cup. After seven years of preparations, taken right down to the wire, and for the first time since 1950, Brazil, the emotional epicentre of 'the beautiful game' would play host to international football's greatest event.

However, for one Brazilian born in the north-east of the country it would be a day to look on and perhaps ask what if. Costa, the man at the centre of the controversy, had indeed made it to the World Cup in his home country. Yet, rather than donning the famous yellow shirt of the *Seleção* and being charged by coach Luiz Felipe Scolari with firing Brazil to a fifth world title, he was busy preparing himself over in Curitiba to try and help his adopted nation and current world champions Spain in their quest to become the first since Pelé's era to retain their crown.

Brazil's 2002 World Cup-winning coach Scolari had only returned to the helm of the national side after the dismissal of previous incumbent Mano Menezes in November 2012. Upon reappointing Scolari, CBF president José Maria Marin outlined the federation's reasons for looking to 'Felipão' and his assistant, 1994 World Cup-winning coach Carlos Alberto Parreira, to inspire a return to past glories:

> After a thorough analysis, thinking about what would be best for Brazilian football and its fans, we have assumed the responsibility to give the squad to Luiz Felipe Scolari and Carlos Alberto Parreira for the World Cup and Confederations Cup. Their experience, track record and history will help Brazil be victorious.

Menezes, himself only in charge for two years since Brazil's second-half World Cup quarter-final capitulation under Dunga at the hands of the Dutch in 2010, departed with a win percentage rate of 64 per cent, with twenty-one victories, six losses and six draws to his name. Having previously coached both Grêmio and Corinthians, Menezes was, during his time in charge of the national team, an advocate of the 'traditional' attacking style of play practised by so many of his predecessors before him. Under Scolari and Dunga, the team had resorted to playing a pragmatic counter-attacking game that was in its very essence un-Brazilian.

There had admittedly been lows, namely the quarter-final defeat on penalties to Paraguay at the 2011 Copa America, and the disappointment of his team only securing the silver medal after defeat to Mexico in the 2012 Olympic final. Yet Menezes had, before his abrupt sacking, overseen a hugely satisfying victory on penalties over Argentina following a 3–3 draw on aggregate to win the *Superclásico de las Américas,* in a match now recognised as Brazil's 1001st official match. South American football expert Tim Vickery in *World Soccer Magazine* quoted 1970 World Cup-winner Tostão in his newspaper column as saying that the decision to axe Menezes was a 'backward step' and that 'in two years he got more right than wrong – mainly getting right a collective idea of play. His team have marked high, taking control of games, kept the ball on the ground with more exchange of passes, which used to be the Brazilian style.'

Upon Scolari's reappointment, Tostão wasn't the only national legend vocally unimpressed with the decision of the Brazilian Football Federation (CBF). World Cup-winning captain Carlos Alberto Torres, scorer of one of the greatest goals in World Cup history, the last in a 4–1 demolition of Italy in the 1970 final, said: 'A coach who took a team down to the second division should not take over the national team.' He was of course referring to Scolari's dismissal by Palmeiras in September with the club doomed to certain relegation for the second time in ten years.

The derision his appointment met fell on deaf ears, however. 'Big Phil', as he is also known, was back and things would be done his way. Approximately fifteen months ahead of the opening goal of the 2014 World Cup finals, Costa could well have been guilty of sharing the dreams of his fellow countrymen. After finally establishing himself as one of Diego Simeone's key men alongside Radamel Falcao in the Atlético Madrid team, the stage was set for him to make his debut for *La Canarinha*. Having lost the inaugural match of his second spell in charge to Roy Hodgson's England at Wembley in

February, Scolari had finally bowed to populist opinion and called the all-action striker into his squad for the international friendly matches against Italy and Russia in March.

Named as one of five forwards included in the squad alongside Neymar, Lucas Moura, Hulk and Fred, Costa was understandably ecstatic and proud upon hearing the news of his maiden call-up, commenting: 'I do not know what to say, I don't have the words. It's a dream I've had all my life and now it has come true. I don't believe it yet. I'm very happy. This is made possible by God. I'm on cloud nine.'

He believed his dreams were about to come true. He was ready to follow in the footsteps of his idol, the Brazilian Ronaldo. All the disappointments, numerous loan spells and hard work and determination had been worth it. He had arrived at his goal and with just over a year to go until the biggest festival of football witnessed in the country in more than half a century kicked off, Costa was overcome with gratitude towards Scolari: 'He called to ask if I would play with the national team and I said it was a dream for me. He said he would call me one day and he was following me. It was a surprise.'

Indeed, not since Ronaldo, who retired from the international set-up after the 2006 World Cup, had Brazil possessed a truly world-class centre forward playing at the very highest level. Adriano, a member of that same 2006 squad, had possessed the ability but not the consistency to fill the hole left by *el fenómeno*'s retirement. Luís Fabiano had scored three goals for Brazil at the World Cup in South Africa but had gone off the boil somewhat since his return from Seville to Brazilian club football with São Paulo, whereas Fred and Jô, both back in Brazil after underwhelming spells in Europe, were regarded by many as substandard for the coveted role of central striker for the *Seleção*.

Of course there was still the ubiquitous Neymar, but the ridiculously talented Barcelona forward would need quality assistance if Brazil were to land a record sixth world title. Many regarded Costa as the perfect choice to partner the country's great hope, yet quizzed on whether he would have had a decision to make if Spain's Vicente del Bosque called him up, Costa, while not completely ruling out the possibility, preferred to stay diplomatic and reaffirm his joy at his selection for the country of his birth: 'I am very pleased and happy because it is my country, but Spain has given me everything in football. If the call came too I would be proud, but now is the happiest moment of my career and I'm happy with Brazil.'

Strangely, Scolari resisted the temptation to throw Costa into the lion's den from the referee's first whistle against old rivals Italy in Geneva, Switzerland. Choosing to start with an attacking trio of Neymar, Hulk and Fred, Costa had to wait until the sixty-eighth minute to enter the fray after the *Azzurri* had fought back from a 2–0 half-time deficit to draw level in the second half. It appeared a strange decision not to start Costa given his consistent club form and the fact that just four days earlier he had scored a brace for Atlético against Osasuna in Pamplona to keep their bid for a second-placed finish behind Barcelona but above city rivals Real Madrid still alive. In addition, his direct opponent for the central striking berth, Fred, was playing for Fluminense in the Rio state championship, a poor standard of competition when compared to Spain's La Liga and the Brazilian national championship, which wasn't due to commence until late May.

Yet, somewhat ironically it was Fred who pounced to open the scoring at the back post before Oscar, Costa's future team-mate at Chelsea, doubled the lead before the break. Danielle De Rossi pulled one back nine minutes after the restart and three minutes later Mario Balotelli curled home a wonderful shot to draw the Italians level. After entering the fray with twenty-two minutes of the match remaining, Costa's debut proved a low-key introduction to international football as Brazil held on to draw with the Italians, who had looked the more likely winners in the latter stages of the game.

Scolari's men moved on to London to face Fabio Capello's Russia at Stamford Bridge four days later. Back in familiar territory following an ultimately unhappy six-month spell as Blues boss that had ended with him being sacked in February 2009, Scolari made three changes to his line-up for the *Seleção*'s latest friendly match. And although Hulk was demoted to the bench in favour of Kaká, whose powers were by now clearly not what they once were, almost inexplicably, Costa once again had to be content with a place on the substitutes' bench.

After struggling to break down Capello's stubborn outfit, it was the Italian who was celebrating with seventeen minutes to go after Zenit Saint Petersburg winger Victor Fayzulin drilled home following a goal-mouth scramble. Up until the deadlock was broken, it had looked as if Costa would finish the match where he had begun it, sitting on the bench. But with Brazil trailing, Scolari afforded Costa a paltry twelve minutes to try and find an equaliser on a ground he would be calling his new home wearing the colours of Chelsea in little over a year. It was an equaliser that would arrive too, but not for Costa, as a neat interchange between Marcelo and Hulk, also on from the bench, afforded the previously ineffective Fred an open goal to spare Brazil's and Scolari's blushes.

A squad containing only home-based players defeated Bolivia 4–0 and drew 2–2 at home with Chile in April, and once again Costa's name was conspicuous by its absence after failing to force his way into Scolari's list for the now-traditional World Cup warm-up tournament, the Confederations Cup. Costa could see his World Cup dreams fading fast. Yet his omission wasn't the biggest surprise. Ronaldinho, shining for Atlético Mineiro in the Copa Libertadores, and Real Madrid's Kaká were both notable absentees when the squad was announced despite Scolari intimating that only one of the two would make his list for the eight-team tournament. Neither did in the end.

It wasn't the first time in his long career that Scolari had been at the centre of a controversial debate over his selection policies. Back in 2002, in the run-up to the World Cup, despite Presidential clamour for his inclusion, Scolari omitted legendary striker Romário from his squad to the dismay of just about the whole country. With one Brazilian newspaper branding him 'public enemy number one' and the Brazilian public firmly in thirty-six-year-old Romário's corner, Scolari announced that the striker's decision to pull out of the Copa America squad the year before to have eye surgery, only to postpone the operation in favour of going to Mexico with his club Vasco da Gama, was the reason for his exclusion. Romário, who had averaged more than a goal a game that season for his club, was livid and responded to a congregation of reporters following a Vasco training session:

I can't believe that not going to the Copa América has stopped me from going to the World Cup. Other players didn't go to the Copa and were picked again. It would be better if I were there, but I'm going to get on with my life. My conscience is clear, I'm going to get on with my business here and I hope he [Scolari] does the same there. As he says, I am no use technically or tactically in his view. He's made his choice. I consider myself good enough to be in the squad but the coach doesn't. Now, I'm going to look for strength with my parents, my wife, my children and my friends. The real reason for me not being picked will appear one day.

Back in league action with Atlético, as if to illustrate to Scolari exactly what he was missing, just three days after the squad announcement for the summer tournament Costa showed pace, power and deadly finishing to equalise for Atleti before the team earned a 2–1 victory over José Mourinho's Real in the Copa del Rey final, their first win over their bitter rivals in fourteen years and twenty-five matches.

A prestige friendly against Roy Hodgson's England at the Maracanã followed at the start of June. The clash, the first between the two teams in Brazil since John Barnes' mesmeric wonder goal in the Maracanã in 1984 helped the visitors to a shock 2–0 win, finished 2–2 with Brazil needing a late goal from Paulinho to rescue a draw as Brazil continued to stutter with the Confederations Cup around the corner. Five days later Internacional's promising target man, Leandro Damião, pulled out of the cup squad with a thigh injury, but rather than giving Costa the opportunity to stake his case for a place in the team, Scolari preferred to call up Atlético Mineiro's Jô instead. Jô had benefitted greatly in terms of goals scored for his club from Ronaldinho and Bernard's presence, but realistically he was never going to strike fear into the world's best central defenders.

Brazil eased to a 3–0 friendly victory over France in preparation for the tournament, yet the actual tournament was staged to the backdrop of continual and justified mass protestations taking place on the streets of Brazil in anger at the amount of money being spent on the World Cup as opposed to much-needed improvements in public services. On the pitch, Neymar inspired the team to greater heights than thought imaginable as Brazil cruised past Japan, Mexico and Italy in the group stages to set up an emotional and memory-evoking semi-final against Uruguay. In 1950, Uruguay had caused one of the major shocks in World Cup history when they defeated the favourites Brazil 2–1 in the deciding match at a shell-shocked Maracanã. There were no surprises this time, however, as a late winner from Paulinho ensured progression for the hosts to face world champions Spain in the final.

And despite being second favourites to lift the trophy, Scolari's men produced an outstanding performance to sweep Spain aside 3–0 to win their third consecutive Confederations title, ending La Roja's twenty-nine-match unbeaten record in the process. Although inspired by Neymar, Fred's two-goal haul in the final and five goals in the tournament overall had cemented his place as Scolari's favoured central striker, while late squad replacement Jô had also chipped in with two goals earlier in the tournament to suggest a role as backup to Fred was his for the taking.

## TUG OF WAR

On 5 July 2013, Costa's club Atlético made a far-reaching announcement, when they declared that their Brazilian striker had taken dual citizenship after swearing into the Spanish Constitution in the Civil Registry of Madrid. The move was significant for Simeone's plans for the coming season as it released one of three non-EU spaces Costa had occupied at the club the previous season. It was however a move that was to have further, more controversial implications.

After again being ignored by Scolari for a 1–0 friendly defeat against Switzerland in Basel, Costa started the domestic season like a man possessed. With Falcao departed to megabucks AS Monaco, Costa was now Simeone's main man and the confidence of his club manager showed as Atlético won their opening three games with Costa scoring three in the process. It all led to the inevitable speculation that Vicente del Bosque was considering calling up Costa to his Spanish squad. With the rumours becoming more vocal, Costa's team-mate Filipe Luís, who had been rewarded for a fine season in 2012–13 with a place in Scolari's Confederations Cup squad, insisted that his club team-mates would support him no matter what decision he arrived at: 'Diego is in great form, it is a very difficult decision to have to make; deciding on one country or another is very complicated, but at the same time he is privileged that he has to choose between the two best in the world. Hardly anybody has that opportunity and we are here to support him.'

Again omitted from Scolari's squad in mid-September for the friendlies with Australia and Portugal, Costa's frustration at being constantly ignored by the country of his birth resulted in him playing out of his skin for the Rojiblancos, netting ten goals in the club's first eight matches of the season, with all eight ending in victory and a share of the top spot with Barcelona.

After a luncheon meeting with Spanish supremo Vicente del Bosque in early October 2013, Costa, possessing dual-nationality and a Spanish passport, announced that he was willing to play for La Roja. His revelation seemed to awaken Scolari who had cast the fiery forward aside after affording him a total of just thirty-six minutes in the friendly matches against Italy and Russia earlier in the year. Inexplicably, despite leading the Spanish goalscoring charts ahead of prolific forwards of the stature of Lionel Messi and Cristiano Ronaldo, Costa again missed out on selection for friendlies with South Korea and Zambia in mid-October. Enough was enough, despite Big Phil's insistence on Spanish radio station Cadena Cope in response to a prank caller impersonating Atlético president Enrique Cerezo, that 'If I were to choose the squad for the World Cup today, Costa would be on the list. I love him. He's first on the list.'

The ridiculous situation caused by Scolari's refusal to give him a fair chance to prove his worth had come to a head with just over seven months remaining until the World Cup's commencement. His public courting of the player had come too late. In an almost desperate-sounding address in response to Costa's declaration of loyalty to his adopted nation, Scolari rebuked Spain for their interest in capping the Brazilian:

Spain should respect Brazil's right to choose its players. We intend to pick him again. We want to better analyse him. He is a Brazilian who has been performing well with Atlético Madrid. When Diego played for us the first time we heard about his satisfaction to be defending the colours of Brazil and that's still the case.

Scolari was wrong, and despite calling him up to face Honduras and Chile in Brazil's latest series of friendlies in the USA, on 29 October 2013, Costa confirmed it. In a letter to Brazilian Football Federation secretary general Julio Cesar Avellada and FIFA, the Spanish Football Federation declared that Costa had stated 'his desire to be at the disposition of the Spanish national team manager Vicente del Bosque'.

Wanting to outline his reasons for making the controversial switch, Costa admitted that his time in Spain had enabled him to develop into the person and player he had become:

I hope people understand and respect my decision because it has been very difficult. It was very difficult to choose between the country where you were born and the country that has given you everything. I looked at everything and saw that it was right and best to play for Spain because this is where I have done everything. All that I have in my life was given to me by this country. I hope the people of Brazil understand because it is not something against Brazil. I have family in Brazil and it is the country where I was born. I hope that God allows me to live there again the future.

Del Bosque was understandably delighted. Scolari on the other hand was furious, accusing Costa of 'turning his back on the dream of millions to represent the five-time world champions at the World Cup in Brazil.' Del Bosque had managed to persuade one of the hottest goal scoring talents in world football to commit to representing La Roja. With Spain's record goal scorer David Villa in the home straight of his international days and Fernando Torres no longer the threat he once was, Costa was looking like the answer to del Bosque's prayers for a top-class striker. Addressing his switch of allegiance and his selection of Costa to face minnows Equatorial Guinea and South Africa in mid-November, Del Bosque said:

> He has fulfilled all the requirements to play for Spain and he is in very good form. The last step in the process was to get to know him personally and he left us with a magnificent impression. I have absolutely no doubt he will be a squad member like any other. I expect that a player that fights like Diego with such energy, a player with the quality he has on and off the ball, to be a positive addition.

After happily accepting Spain's invitation, Costa received the support of an unlikely ally when Brazil's greatest ever player, Pelé, spoke glowingly about him and why he had been brave to choose his adopted nation over the country of his birth. Speaking at a marketing event in São Paulo, Diego's former city of residence, Brazil's record goal scorer and three-time world champion, said:

> It's a matter of patriotism. I wanted him to represent Brazil, but maybe he wouldn't have even been in the

starting XI. If he felt discredited in Brazil then his attitude was right. I think we have to respect his decision. He tried to explain that he hasn't been recognised for some time and for that reason took the decision to play for Spain. He was courageous and I understand. He is another player that could have represented Brazil. I have the impression that he made the right decision given that he hasn't been recognised in Brazil.

Although unusual it wasn't an unprecedented situation. Many players had taken advantage of the ruling which stated a person who had lived continuously in a country, without representing his or her home country in a competitive and not friendly fixture, had the legal right to switch allegiances. Costa and Spain had broken no rules. Indeed, he wouldn't be the first Brazilian to represent Spain. In fact he would be the fifth after another former Atleti forward Heraldo Becerra, who won a solitary cap in the 1970s. Catanha gained three caps in 2000, Donato represented Spain at Euro '96 and Marcos Senna won twenty-eight caps and the European Championship with Spain in 2008 under del Bosque's predecessor and Atlético Madrid legend, Luis Aragonés.

Indeed, it was Scolari himself in 2003 who was in charge of the Portuguese national team when Deco, at the time a star in the FC Porto midfield under José Mourinho, emerged from the substitutes' bench for his debut to score the winner from a free kick against the country of his birth, Brazil. Deco's presence in Scolari's 2004 European Championship squad wasn't universally popular either and provoked the team's star attraction Luís Figo to criticise his team-mate's inclusion, saying: 'If you're born Chinese, well, you have to play for China,' to which the attacking midfielder retorted: 'I was born in Brazil and it would be a lie to say that I'm Portuguese now and not Brazilian. But I love Portugal and I love playing for the national team.'

Scolari would also go on to give Brazilian-born Pepe his debut for Portugal in 2007, a player Costa would go on to enjoy numerous physical battles on the opposing sides of the Madrid divide. Frustratingly for Costa, after suffering a muscle injury in training with Atlético, he was forced to pull out of the squad for the matches with Equatorial Guinea and South Africa and subsequently postpone his debut for La Roja.

However, his incredible goalscoring feats for Atlético ensured there was no chance he would be discarded by Del Bosque before he had been given an opportunity to show what he could do. Del Bosque had got his man. He wasn't about to let a minor injury deprive him of a world-class striker. And, after twenty-one goals in twenty-six league outings and twenty-seven goals in total for the season, Costa was once again called into the squad in early March for the national team's last outing on European soil before the World Cup kicked off in June. Ironically, Costa's second international debut would be against the country he had made his first international debut against a year earlier: Italy. And it would be on familiar territory, with the Estadio Vicente Calderón, Atlético's home, providing the backdrop to his debut. Reflecting upon his selection, Costa admitted to cable television station Canal Plus show *Espacio Reservado* that Del Bosque had made him feel wanted with his honesty:

I never imagined [that his decision would attract such attention]. When I realised there was interest from Spain I started to imagine things, and thought 'Why not?' It is a privilege that the world champions want you to play for them, especially given the quality of players they have. I felt very important. I value it a lot. Vicente del Bosque showed me the person that he is. I like to talk with people face-to-face, I feel the truth and lies, and Vicente was very clear. He didn't promise me anything. I don't like it when people promise me things, I like to earn it. This I value.

Atlético colleagues Koke and Juanfran joined him in the squad for the match at their home stadium, and a goal from Barcelona winger Pedro just past the hour was enough to seal a winning start to Costa's Spain career. Unlike twelve months earlier, Costa played from the kick-off and completed the full ninety minutes. And although it proved to be a low-key introduction to international football with his adopted nation, he did show some nice touches and exchanges throughout to give Del Bosque encouragement that he could adapt his game from the counter-attacking system adopted at Atlético to the possession-based game practised by Spain. After the final whistle former Real Madrid coach Del Bosque enthused: 'It's good news. Little by little he's getting into the team dynamic. There isn't a single player who could be harmful for the play of Spain.'

Speaking after a winning debut, despite being unable to open his account on home soil, a happy Costa thanked his team-mates and the supporters for their backing:

The dream debut was to score a goal. It wasn't to be but I feel very happy. I thank my colleagues and the fans for the treatment given to me. It feels like I've been playing with them for quite some time. I felt comfortable. I now have to focus only on Atlético Madrid, where I have to do a good job to be able to return to the [Spanish] squad. People know that I am Brazilian, but my desire was to play with Spain. The love given to me won't be forgotten.

Returning to action in La Liga, Costa set about inspiring Atlético towards Primera División and European glory and by the end of March 2014, Simeone's men were topping the La Liga table and awaiting a mouth-watering Champions League quarter-final with Barcelona. However, after just thirty minutes of the first leg tie with Barca at the Camp Nou, Simeone was forced into an early substitution when Costa limped off with a muscle strain. Atlético came away from the match with a priceless away goal and a 1–1 draw to take back to the Vicente Calderón. After missing a 1–0 victory over Villarreal and the return fixture with the Catalans, which Atlético won 1–0 to progress to the semi-finals, Costa returned to the starting line-up for the next fixture away at Getafe. And he displayed typical tenacity and commitment to the cause when scoring the crucial second goal in a 2–0 win – brutally injuring himself in the process as he collided with an upright. The collision left him writhing in pain on the floor with his shin streaming with blood. However, Simeone allayed concerns the injury could rule him out of Atlético's remaining matches and possibly the upcoming World Cup in his post-match press conference.

Yet, worryingly for del Bosque, after helping Atlético to

knock his future employers Chelsea out of the Champions League at the semi-final stage, Costa lasted just fourteen minutes of the title-winning draw against Barcelona at the Camp Nou and only nine minutes of the final against Real Madrid in Lisbon. Once again he was forced to limp off early when he suffered a reoccurrence of a muscle injury that would curtail his involvement in a final Atlético would lead until the ninety-fourth minute before finally succumbing to their great rivals 4–1.

Despite his injury woes, Del Bosque was prepared to wait for Costa and give him the time to take his place in the final squad for the World Cup. It was a huge confidence boost for the physical striker. Barely a year earlier, as Brazil triumphantly lifted the Confederations Cup in Rio, playing at the World Cup would have seemed a distant dream to Costa. But twelve months on and here was Del Bosque declaring that Spain would give him all the time he needed to recover. Speaking to Spanish radio network Cadena SE, del Bosque, who had delayed naming his twenty-three-man squad, said:

Diego has got a muscular injury, we're monitoring him closely and keeping an eye on how it evolves. We will wait until the last minute before making our decision. We're not doing this on a whim – we have until June 2 to submit the list of twenty-three players and so we have no reason to be hasty. I really hope he makes it.

Perhaps worried that Costa would recover in time to fire Spain to ultimate glory in his homeland, Brazil boss Scolari was quoted in Spanish newspaper *AS* as saying he would have taken the prolific forward to the World Cup as part of his final twenty-three. However, Costa was having none of it, rejecting Scolari's claims that he had spoken with the forward twice about him playing for Brazil at the summer's showpiece event: 'Scolari never called me by telephone. The only coach that I spoke with was Del Bosque, who showed interest in me, invited me for a meal and made me realise that I was in his plans. I am Brazilian and that is not going to change, but I want to win the World Cup with Spain.'

After defeating Bolivia 2–0 in their penultimate warm-up match, on 31 May Del Bosque put an end to all the conjecture surrounding Costa's fitness when he announced his highly anticipated squad to the world. As expected, Atlético's talisman had recovered sufficiently to take his place alongside fellow forwards David Villa and Chelsea's Fernando Torres, seeing off the challenge from Manchester City's Álvaro Negredo and Juventus' Fernando Llorente in the process.

To prove his fitness, Costa was selected to face El Salvador in Spain's final match before their campaign kicked off against 2010 losing finalists Holland. And within three minutes of the game kicking off, Costa had drawn a penalty from the El Salvador defence, only to watch Fàbregas balloon his effort from the spot high over the bar. After a goalless first hour and with the match still finely poised, a Sergio Ramos header back across the six-yard area enabled substitute Villa to nod home just ahead of Costa who was waiting in the wings to pounce for his first goal in the red shirt of Spain.

Villa, added a second to add some gloss to the victory but more importantly Costa lasted seventy-four minutes of the match to alleviate concerns surrounding his fitness. And following his first competitive match in just over a month, Costa admitted it was good to blow away the cobwebs and build his fitness up in anticipation of Spain's tournament opener just seven days later:

> I needed the game against El Salvador. Before that I felt OK, but I relapsed. Now I'm fine, and there won't be a problem with the first match. It's normal to feel [anxiety]. We're training to get better and be at our peak fitness. The climate will take its toll, because we play most of our season in the winter. It's important the pitches are well watered. Things are going well. I've been treated as I hoped. I've been supported by a lot of people who understand what happened. My parents are really happy I'm here, close to them. They support my decision.

Ahead of the big kick-off, Brazil's legendary number 10 and World Cup ambassador Pelé spoke to *AS* about Costa's inclusion in the Spanish squad, revealing that he held no grudges against the forward for choosing to represent his adopted nation, while also stressing that he hoped the decision would not come back to haunt Brazil:

> It surprises me to the extent that before nobody would have given up the chance of playing for Brazil. But times have changed. And the main thing is to respect his decision. He needs to be where he feels comfortable and that's with Spain. He had the chance to do it because he's got dual nationality and the only thing I want now is that he's not lucky against Brazil.

To the backdrop of mass public protestations around the country, Brazil recovered from a one-goal deficit against Croatia in São Paulo to get their World Cup as host nation off to a winning start. The whole of Brazil rejoiced. However, any notion that a good opening-day result for the country of his birth would translate to a less vitriolic homecoming for himself the next day were quickly dispelled when Costa entered the field of play for Spain's opening Group B match against the Netherlands.

Selected to start the match at Salvador's Arena Fonte Nova, 300 kilometres south of his hometown of Lagarto, Costa emerged from the tunnel to a poisonous chorus of jeers and heckling. In the eyes of Brazilians up and down the country he was a traitor. But it had been expected. Costa had been fully aware of the type of welcome home he was likely to receive. He would have been naïve not to. Del Bosque's Spain, the holders, were up against Louis van Gaal's Dutch outfit. But, this was a very different proposition to 2010, when La Roja had beaten Bert van Marwijk's overly physical team in extra time thanks to Andres Iniesta's winning strike.

Having seen Brazil ignite the tournament with their Neymar-inspired win over Niko Kovač's plucky Croatian side, Costa was understandably hoping to get his own World Cup off to a winning start against the Dutch, who themselves were aiming to make amends for that defeat at Soccer City Stadium in Johannesburg four years earlier. Costa was selected, despite ongoing fitness concerns, to lead the Spanish attack in Salvador ahead of Spain's record goalscorer David Villa and Chelsea's Fernando Torres. Unlike two years before in the final of Euro 2012, when they had employed Cesc Fàbregas in the false number nine role, Del Bosque wanted the man whose twenty-seven goals had inspired Atlético Madrid to their first La Liga title in eighteen years in the team. Elsewhere, Del Bosque had gone for experience in his line-up, retaining seven of the team that had won the final in 2010.

Amid the deafening crescendo of derision that greeted him every time the ball came within close proximity, Costa, making his World Cup debut, had started the match looking nervous with a succession of uncertain touches. After falling foul of a crunching early tackle from his equally tenacious marker, Ron Vlaar, he did get the better of the Aston Villa stopper on one occasion only to skew his shot horribly wide of Jasper Cillessen's goal. Ten minutes later, however, Costa atoned for his earlier miss when he latched onto Xavi's brilliant defence-splitting pass before being felled in the area under Stefan de Vrij's challenge. The referee Nicola Rizzoli pointed to the spot. Replays poured scorn on the penalty award; Costa was shown to have stood on the Feyenoord defender's outstretched leg as he turned inside the challenge. However, de Vrij's reckless attempt to tackle Costa had given Spain the chance of a lead.

Xabi Alonso's assured spot kick past Cillessen put La Roja ahead. Costa had played his part. Things were looking good for del Bosque's men and they nearly added to their advantage when David Silva missed a great chance to put them two up when his chipped effort from Iniesta's pass was saved by Cillessen. Spain were beginning to exert pressure, but one minute before the interval Robin van Persie's fabulous improvised diving header from Daley Blind's superb 50-metre cross-field pass left Spain's static defence and goalkeeper Iker Casillas stranded to level the game going into the break.

Soon after the resumption of play, the Dutch took the lead when Blind again split the Spanish defence to allow Arjen Robben to fire home for 2–1. By now Robben was running riot and minutes later his dangerous run at the heart of the defence allowed van Persie to smash his shot against Casillas' bar. A lucky escape. And with just over an hour played the World Champions were still losing. Del Bosque, looking to switch the momentum of the match back in his team's favour, made two changes with Torres replacing Costa and Pedro taking over from Alonso as La Roja went on the attack.

Costa's constant barracking from the vociferous crowd was over for the day. But things were to get far worse for Del Bosque and his men. De Vrij headed home from a tight angle to make it 3–1, despite protests from Casillas that he had been impeded in the build-up to the goal. And Spain's record-appearance maker's misery was compounded when he attempted to dribble a back pass past van Persie, only for the Manchester United forward to dispossess him and roll the ball into an empty net for 4–1. It was getting embarrassing now. But things were to get still worse. With ten minutes remaining and with the Spanish falling to pieces all over the pitch, Robben ghosted through before teasing Casillas and hammering his shot into the top corner for 5–1. The Dutch supporters were delirious, the travelling Spanish inconsolable. A terrible day for Costa and his team-mates was over. They could still qualify for the knockout stages if they beat Chile and Australia, but would they be able to recover from such a beating?

After all, Spain hadn't conceded five goals in a match for over half a century and not since a 6–1 hammering from

Brazil in 1950 had they conceded five or more goals in a World Cup match. If they wanted to defend their title, they would have to recover quickly. After the drubbing at the hands of the Dutch, Costa admitted to the press after the final whistle that the match had been a disaster but promised that he and his team-mates would learn from the defeat and come back stronger:

> Nobody likes to lose and even less in this way but people know that we can't give up because we have lots of possibilities. We must learn from defeats and they can serve us as a lesson so that it doesn't happen again. We have options. The good thing in life is that there is always an opportunity, we have to take advantage of this and fight right to the end. I am very happy and content for my first World Cup. It's not been the start that I wanted but it is necessary to take the good things [from the situation]. I will give everything for this shirt. If we are all united together we can advance the cause and make people as happy as before.

In the day's other match Chile had defeated Australia 3–1 at the Arena Pantanal in Cuiabá. For Spain it meant defeat in their second match against Chile at the Maracanã in Rio de Janeiro was unthinkable. If they lost they would be going home. Del Bosque kept faith with Costa for the clash at Brazil's iconic stadium despite his inauspicious hour in Salvador. Meanwhile, La Roja's experienced man at the helm dropped Xavi in favour of his Barcelona team-mate Pedro as the team went in search of a victory that would keep their qualification hopes alive, while another Catalonian, Gerard Piqué, dropped out in favour of Javi Martínez in the Spanish rear guard.

Having defeated the South Americans 1–0 en route to winning the World Cup back in 2010, Spain were acutely aware that this was a Chilean team brimming with confidence and style in the form of Juventus's midfield extraordinaire Arturo Vidal and forward Alexis Sánchez, who would take his place in the Premier League with Arsenal after the finals. But it was Costa – another South American forward who would also be moving to London after the finals – who would carve out the first real opportunity of the match. Running menacingly at the retreating Chilean defence, Costa, still the victim of heavy jeering from the crowd, opened up a shooting opportunity for himself only to drag his shot wide of the goal.

However, it would be Chile who would gain the upper hand twenty minutes in when Sánchez seized on a poor pass from Alonso to feed Charles Aránguiz in the area, and his pass square to Eduardo Vargas was finished expertly by the forward to put Chile 1–0 ahead. Spain were wobbling badly and before half-time they were two goals down when Casillas' poor parry of Sánchez's free kick fell to Aránguiz who fired home the rebound.

Costa spurned a glorious opportunity to get Spain back in the match in the second half when he saw his shot blocked at the last moment, and the much-maligned forward turned provider shortly after when his acrobatic overhead kick enabled Sergio Busquets to somehow conspire to miss from only a few yards out. Needing a draw at the very least to avoid becoming the fifth defending champions to be knocked out in the group stage, Del Bosque sacrificed Costa just past the hour mark for Torres, but despite late efforts from Andrés Iniesta and Santi Cazorla, Spain, the reigning World champions, were out and on their way home. It had been an awful World Cup for the team. For Costa it was a sad end to a great year. And although Spain would go on to beat Australia 3–0 in their final match in Curitiba, a match Costa would watch from the bench, it would be too little too late for Spain.

In the aftermath of Spain's unexpected elimination, midfielder Xabi Alonso came out and questioned the squad's hunger and ambition in the press. However, speaking to Spanish newspaper *Marca*, Costa strongly refuted his team-mate's claims: 'I don't agree with his comments. Everybody here was focused on winning. I'm here because I wanted to win, I wanted to reach the final and do a good job, but it wasn't to be. We obviously lacked something, but in terms of quality we're superior to many other teams.'

As for Costa's country of birth, an impressive run, which saw them overcome South American opposition twice in the form of Chile and Colombia on their way to the semi-finals, came to an abrupt and brutal end for Scolari when eventual champions Germany massacred the hosts 7–1 at a shocked Maracanã before claiming an extra-time victory over Lionel Messi's Argentina in the final.

On signing for Chelsea shortly after the World Cup, Costa spoke about his and the squad's disappointment at their group-stage exit to the club's official website in his first interview since his arrival from Atlético Madrid:

To say the World Cup didn't go well for Spain is an understatement but that's something we need to put to the back of our minds and forget about, the players need to move forward. I went into the tournament after missing a month with a hamstring injury but now I've been able to have a good holiday and I feel much better. I'm looking forward to this next chapter in my career. I want to keep pushing myself and improving as a player.

He wouldn't have to wait long for the opportunity to try and exorcise his World Cup demons either. Three Premier League matches, in fact. And having hit the ground running with four goals in an impressive start to his new career in west London, Costa, now back to full fitness after his struggles at the World Cup, went into the friendly with France at the Stade de France in early September looking sharp and refreshed. But despite putting in a vastly improved performance, Spain, sporting a number of changes to the team following the retirements of Xavi and Xabi Alonso, crashed to a 1–0 defeat. And it was a familiar face for Costa who did the damage. His new club team-mate Loïc Rémy, bought by José Mourinho to be his understudy, fired home the winning goal on seventy-four minutes after entering the field of play from the substitutes' bench. However, Costa's night had already come to end before Remy's intervention, the forward having limped off after sixty-seven minutes with yet another hamstring injury.

The injury would rule him out of Spain's first match on the road to defending their European Championship crown in France, as they strolled past Macedonia 5–1 in his absence. Costa returned to the Spain squad for the next two qualifiers in October. But his return to the starting line-up alongside

Valencia's Paco Alcácer, a complete change from the tika-taka philosophy of years gone by, ended in massive disappointment, when Slovakia caused a huge upset as they defeated Spain 2–1 in Žilina.

Costa, with nine goals already in the English Premier League, looked dangerous throughout the match and flashed a header just wide in the first half before Slovakian goalkeeper Matúš Kozáčik parried his point-blank header away from goal on the stroke of half-time. Kozáčik also made a fine save from Costa in the second half following a trademark run and low shot to preserve his country's one-goal advantage, and despite Alcácer's equaliser eight minutes from time, Slovakia grabbed a shock victory at the death thanks to a header from former Chelsea youngster Miroslav Stoch. The result sent shockwaves around Europe, with Spain's incredible eight-year and thirty-six-game unbeaten qualifying record having come to an abrupt end.

Four days later, however, del Bosque's men had the perfect opportunity to get their qualifying hopes back on track with a trip to face Luxembourg. Perennially the whipping boys of any qualifying group, it would be the perfect opportunity for Costa to break his scoring duck in his seventh international for Spain. And so it proved, but not before an excruciatingly difficult first forty-five minutes for the Chelsea forward, which would see him miss a whole host of chances to get off the mark for La Roja.

Goals from David Silva and Alcácer put the double European champions ahead at the break and in the sixty-ninth minute, following some pinball in the penalty area from a short free kick, the moment arrived. Turning with his back to goal, Costa fired home from six yards to warrant emotional celebrations with every Spanish outfield player rushing to congratulate him. He had finally done what Del Bosque brought him into the Spanish squad to do: score goals. Bayern Munich left back Juan Bernat added gloss to the victory with two minutes remaining, but the night belonged to Costa, who told Spanish television station RTVE after the match of his relief at finally getting his long-awaited goal after playing seven matches for his adopted nation:

> It was bothering me. It played on my mind and the team lost last week, which also really bothered me. This goal has given me new life. The ball broke loose and I just had to force it in. I have to thank the coach for his support. With every game he gave me a new opportunity.

Del Bosque acknowledged the frustration had been building:

> We were all suffering and we were all pleased for Diego Costa because he has worked hard. Now we need to look forward knowing that he will be an important player for us. At half-time I told him to be calm. We all noticed he was a bit nervous, dissatisfied, as he wasn't finding a way through. But when a player has so much desire he will always get there in the end.

Costa would miss out on Spain's latest qualifying victories over Belarus and the Ukraine in November and March, but assuming Spain qualify for the finals in France in 2016, his name will undoubtedly be one of Del Bosque's first picks in the squad. Brazil's loss has most definitely been Spain's gain despite his somewhat slow and complicated start to life as La Roja's main man.

## CHAPTER 11

# FORWARD
# THINKING

'I have met so many wonderful characters in football
and it's difficult to find one better than Diego. Nobody has
given him anything in his life.'
Blues manager José Mourinho reveals his admiration
for new signing Costa

A fter a disappointing and trophy-less conclusion to the
2013–14 campaign, and having completed the majority
of his squad adjustments in the early part of the summer
transfer window, Chelsea manager José Mourinho and his
star-studded squad travelled to Carinthia in southern Austria
to begin their initial preparations for the 2014–15 season.
The training camp would also see them face opposition from
Austrian Bundesliga club Wolfsberger AC as well as a short
trip to neighbouring Slovenia to face NK Olimpija Ljubljana
in the country's capital city. And following Costa's big money
move from Atlético to west London, after Mourinho instructed
the Blues to activate the prolific markman's release clause
of £32 million, Diego, who left Madrid as a hero to Atleti's
adoring fans after firing them to a first league title in eighteen

years, joined fellow big-name signings Cesc Fàbregas and Filipe Luís as part of a squad of twenty-six to head off on the club's first tour of the pre-season. However, the two Spanish internationals would have to wait for their first appearances in the famous royal blue as Mourinho's men played out a satisfactory 1–1 draw against Wolfsberger AC without them.

Two days after the club's opening pre-season friendly, a returning club legend was presented to the assembled media as Mourinho continued to put together a stellar squad in preparation for the forthcoming campaign. Didier Drogba, scorer of what is widely considered by most Chelsea fans to be the most important goal in the club's history with his 2012 Champions League-winning penalty in the shootout victory over Bayern Munich in the Germans' own stadium, signed a one-year contract to return to the Bridge after his contract with Turkish giants Galatasaray expired.

Brought in to provide competition, but more likely cover, for Chelsea's new star forward Diego Costa, Drogba, clearly delighted to be returning to West London to team up with Mourinho once again after two years away, said:

It was an easy decision – I couldn't turn down the opportunity to work with Jose again. Everyone knows the special relationship I have with this club and it has always felt like home to me. My desire to win is still the same and I look forward to the opportunity to help this team. I am excited for this next chapter of my career.

And an equally delighted Mourinho explained his reasoning for bringing the veteran striker back to the club, in the process refuting any suggestions of it being a sentimental recruitment:

> He's coming because he's one of the best strikers in Europe. I know his personality very well and I know if he comes back he's not protected by history or what he's done for this club previously. He is coming with the mentality to make more history.

With the squad further boosted by the addition of the club's fourth all-time top goal scorer, Mourinho unleashed Costa for his debut from the kick-off against Slovenian top-flight club NK Olimpija Ljubljana at the Stožice stadium alongside fellow Spanish international Fernando Torres. After falling behind to a first-half goal from the Slovenians and coming close on a few occasions to a debut goal, ten minutes into the second half, Costa, latching onto a pinpoint through ball from fellow debutant Fàbregas, strode purposefully through the centre of the opposition defence before unleashing an unstoppable shot into the roof of the goal. It was evidence, if any was needed, of the sort of partnership the Chelsea faithful could look forward to between the duo in the upcoming campaign. Minutes later, Kurt Zouma, the club's highly sought-after January purchase from French club St. Etienne, notched the winner from a close-range rebound to give Mourinho his first victory pre-season, before the club departed Austria and Slovenia en route to Arnhem in the Netherlands for the second leg of the club's tour.

In the aftermath of the victory in the Slovenian capital, Mourinho attempted to downplay the high expectations placed upon his new goal poacher and chief assists provider, saying: 'Obviously it's nice for a striker to score in his first game. It's nice, no more than that. For Cesc, it's also important to understand the team, which he is doing step by step.'

Ahead of the clash with Vitesse at the GelreDome in Arnhem, Mourinho sanctioned the sale of forward Romelu Lukaku to Everton. The Belgian international, who had spent the previous two seasons on loan at West Bromwich Albion and Everton respectively, joined the Merseyside club on a permanent basis for a whopping £28 million, as Mourinho continued to adhere to UEFA's Financial Fair Play (FFP) regulations.

The match itself proved a walk in the park for the Blues as they ran out comfortable 3–1 winners. Costa's impressive start to life in Chelsea blue continued when he unselfishly provided goals for Mohamed Salah and Nemanja Matić, sandwiching a wonderful first-half curling free kick from Fàbregas. And after the match, Mourinho expressed his delight and gratitude to the board for allowing him to put together such a formidable squad, while playfully hinting that his business for the summer, with a month of the transfer window remaining, was already at an end:

We have the squad we want and, I repeat, the club was fantastic in the way they worked so hard and so fast to get Diego [Costa], Filipe [Luís] and [Cesc] Fàbregas. Thibaut [Courtois] to return was something obvious. Kurt Zouma we did six months ago. We are happy, and we trust them. We did the job very well. We are outside the market now.

Despite a strong line-up featuring new arrivals Courtois and Drogba, a resounding 3–0 defeat to Werder Bremen at the Weserstadion in north-west Germany followed before the club travelled to the Turkish capital Istanbul to face two forty-five-minute run-outs against Fenerbahçe and Beşiktaş. In the first match against reigning Superliga champions Fenerbahce, a wonderful solo goal from Costa, eluding five defenders on his way to coolly sliding the ball home and a tap-in from Branislav Ivanović ensured a winning start to the three-team tournament. However, a rash and dangerous two-footed lunge from Fenerbahçe's Portuguese defender Bruno Alves, which Costa narrowly avoided, led to Chelsea's explosive striker justifiably losing his cool before being restrained by his team-mates, something fans of his previous clubs had witnessed before.

A late goal in a 1–0 defeat in the second match against Beşiktaş preceded the club's trip to the Hungarian capital Budapest to take part in the opening of Ferencvárosi's brand new Groupama Arena. With just a week remaining before the opening matches of the Barclays Premier League, Chelsea fell behind to a first-half goal in Hungary before goals from Ramires and Fàbregas turned the match on its head.

Following the completion of a testing pre-season programme encompassing six different countries, the Blues returned home to their Cobham training base to prepare for their final friendly against Real Sociedad from the Basque Country. Stamford Bridge played host to its only pre-season match against the team from San Sebastián and it was left to Costa to introduce himself to the Chelsea faithful in the best possible way. Two goals in the first eight minutes of the match finished with typical aplomb left the fans licking their lips ahead of the Premier League kick-off and full of confidence for the team's chances of winning some silverware following a campaign without any the previous season.

After the game's conclusion, a contented Mourinho outlined his satisfaction with his new striker's performance, describing him as a £32 million bargain:

> Diego is a team player who works hard, he's not just about goals. It's about his defensive work, mentality and ambition. This is the player we bought and we were waiting for since last season. This is why we didn't buy a striker in the winter market. We were waiting for him, we have him and hopefully everything goes well. He looks adapted to the team, and the Premier League, not just Chelsea, should be happy. Sometimes we lose important players going to other countries and sometimes we bring new top players here. You can consider that [a bargain] because the market is crazy and the values are very high. For a striker like him, a champion in Spain, a Champions League finalist, a twenty-five-year-old, we consider the price was very much in our favour.

The opening weekend of the Premier League season pitted Mourinho and his team up against Sean Dyche's newly promoted Burnley at Turf Moor, a potential banana skin in the offing. On the first Monday night football of the new season, Mourinho handed full debuts to Courtois, ahead of the long-serving and dependable Petr Čech, and Fàbregas, with the attacking triumvirate of Eden Hazard, Oscar and

World Cup winner André Schürrle in support of the team's third newcomer, Costa.

Yet, any preconceptions that Chelsea would blow away their opponents from Lancashire – back in the big time after five seasons away – proved misguided as the Clarets rocked their high-profile visitors after just thirteen minutes with a stunning strike on the half volley from Scott Arfield. The lead was to prove short-lived however. Just three minutes later a low cross from Ivanović on the right deflected off the far post and fell at the feet of Costa who duly hammered home the equaliser via a slight deflection with his weaker left foot. It had taken the big man just sixteen minutes to open his Chelsea account, an ominous marker of things to come.

Schürrle added a second shortly after with a goal indicative of the imagination flowing throughout Mourinho's team. And after a threatening run from Hazard created space for the marauding Ivanović out wide once again, his centre to Fàbregas was met by a sublime first-time pass from the Spaniard leaving the Burnley defence flat-footed and allowing Schürrle to stroke the ball home unchallenged.

Chelsea should have been two goals clear shortly after when home keeper Tom Heaton felled the dangerous Costa in the box after the striker had escaped the clutches of his markers with an impressive turn of speed. However, to Costa's and Mourinho's dismay, it was the striker and not Heaton who was penalised as referee Michael Oliver yellow-carded the Chelsea forward for perceived simulation. The third goal wasn't long in coming nevertheless, when the impressive Ivanović, so dangerous from set pieces, rose highest from a corner to give Chelsea an unassailable 3–1 lead and a comfortable opening-day victory. After an impressive and goalscoring debut, Mourinho defended his new striker, insisting Oliver and his assistants had made the wrong call to penalise Costa on his debut and not Burnley's goalkeeper:

> Costa last season had a fantastic season and I think in the Spanish league he got five or six yellow cards all season. We all explained to him what people like and don't like in the Premier League, and what people want at Chelsea. He presented himself here today with a fantastic attitude, a competitive attitude, but clean and polite. He had a clear penalty but he got no penalty and he got a yellow card. He was obviously frustrated so I hope he doesn't get more unfair decisions. [Michael] Oliver had a very good game and unfortunately his linesman didn't support him well in that situation.

Five days later, Chelsea fronted up to another Premier League newcomer as Nigel Pearson's Leicester City travelled to West London for the Blues and Costa's first home match of the new season. With Stamford Bridge packed to the rafters on a glorious summer's afternoon and the club's vocal and faithful supporters anticipating a winning start at home to the campaign, the Foxes, arriving on the back of an opening day draw with Everton, proved a tough nut to crack.

Almost inevitably though, it was Ivanović who turned provider, when the right back's penetrating run and cross was chested down by Costa who blasted home just past the hour from close-range to take his tally to two goals in his first two games. A great start to his new career in blue. Belgian winger Hazard added a second late on after a mazy dribble to secure the victory and a maximum six points against two of the league's newly promoted teams. In his post-match press conference, Mourinho described Costa's rapid acclimatisation to English football as seamless: 'I got the feeling in pre-season his adaptation wouldn't be a big deal; he's a happy guy, not speaking good English but always communicating. His style of play is adapted to our needs.'

Further to Mourinho's praise of the former Atlético Madrid striker, legendary club captain John Terry, who had experience of his new team-mate first- hand after coming face-to-face with Costa in the Champions League semi-final the previous season, backed up his manager's praise, explaining his integration in the dressing room despite the obvious language barrier:

Diego scored goals in pre-season and he's been unbelievable in training. He's one of those that you want to be on your side when the bibs are handed out. I knew he was a very good player but I didn't realise how good until I played against him in the Champions League. He's a real handful and he can play. He can get it, he can turn, he's quick, he's powerful and more importantly he can score goals. He's in the right place at the right time. He's been great around the dressing room without speaking any English at all. He's funny because he gets on with everyone and people translate and help out. He's really settled in off the pitch and the goals obviously help too.

Sunday 24 August 2015 was to prove a sad day for all members of the Chelsea family when news of Lord (Richard)

Attenborough's passing filtered through. The club's Life President and ardent Blues fan, famed for his work as an actor, producer and director, passed away at the age of ninety. John Terry described him not only as 'a huge Chelsea fan, but also a tremendous man.'

A favourable Champions League draw later in the week in Monaco saw Chelsea paired with German giants FC Schalke 04, whom the Blues had beaten comfortably both home and away in the group stages the previous season. Slovenian champions NK Maribor and Portuguese giants Sporting Lisbon would also provide opposition in a group that Chelsea would be expected to breeze through, in a competition that Costa had come so close to winning with Atleti in Lisbon the previous May.

With the end of the summer transfer window approaching rapidly, Chelsea announced the departure of Fernando Torres to AC Milan on a two-year loan deal with the Spaniard having returned a disappointing 46 goals in 172 games since his record £50 million arrival from Liverpool in January 2011. Torres, despite winning a number of trophies since his arrival at the club, departed Stamford Bridge as a perceived failure in the media to rival former Chelsea's flops Adrian Mutu, Mateja Kežman and Andriy Shevchenko before him.

Everton provided the next obstacle as Mourinho's men travelled to the north-west looking to end August with a 100 per cent record intact. A thrilling match ensued and the clinical Costa took just thirty-five seconds to open the scoring when he drove his shot through the legs of Tim Howard after timing his run to perfection to latch onto another Fàbregas pass. Things soon got worse for Roberto Martinez's Toffees when Ivanović beat the offside trap to put Chelsea two up with just three minutes on the clock. Kevin Mirallas' superb header on the stroke of half-time got Everton back in the game but Seamus Coleman's own goal restored the away team's two-goal cushion before Steven Naismith soon cut the deficit to a solitary goal once more. Matić's low drive from the edge of the area made it 4–2 before Samuel Eto'o, discarded by Mourinho at the end of the 2013–14 campaign, headed home to make it 4–3 in an end-to-end thriller. Ramires made it 5–3 and in the final minute Costa again showed neat footwork to wrap up the match as his low left-footed drive sealed the points.

After the resounding victory, Mourinho, who had earlier lamented his team's defensive lapses, purred at Costa's work ethic but also expressed his disappointment at perceived gamesmanship from the Everton players, who, he suspected, were trying to get his striker into trouble with the officials during the match:

> He produced a fantastic performance in every aspect. I remember in the first half he was tackling Coleman on the edge of our box. He recovered balls, he held the ball up, and he was aggressive. He came face-to-face with Howard three times and he scored two goals. Howard made a good save in the beginning of the second half. His movement, his quality – everything was really good. The only thing I didn't like in this game, apart from some defensive mistakes, was the way some Everton players were trying to give problems to Diego. I don't think this is English football, and I think it's a contradiction with the Everton team because they are a positive side in every

aspect of the game. To be chasing cards with a player that once more had good behaviour, and was just here to play football and to win the match, is disappointing. The end of the story is that Diego is maybe the best player in the league in these first three matches. He is the top scorer, and he has two yellow cards: one against Burnley where he didn't simulate, and today when everybody was chasing him to get him in trouble.

Following the departure of Torres to AC Milan, Mourinho delved into the kitty on transfer deadline day to bolster his frontline options with the purchase of French forward Loïc Rémy from West London rivals Queens Park Rangers for a fee of £10.5 million. Rémy, scorer of fourteen goals in twenty-six league appearances for Newcastle United the previous season, had looked likely to join Liverpool but reports of a failed medical allegedly scuppered the deal, in Chelsea's favour as it eventually turned out.

New boy Rémy and his new team-mates César Azpilicueta, Costa and Fàbregas then headed off to Paris to engage in an international friendly between France and Spain, which the home team would win 1–0 care of Rémy's solitary strike.

Back in England ahead of the home clash with Swansea City, Costa, having notched four goals in three starts in a blistering start to his Chelsea career, accepted his first personal accolade since his move to the English capital with the Barclays Player of the Month award for August. Upon accepting his prize, a humble Costa said:

## FORWARD THINKING

I'm very happy to win this award. It is important to begin well at a new club and I'm pleased with both my start to the season and also the team's, which is the most important thing. I hope to continue scoring goals to help out the team and keep making our fantastic supporters happy. I thank my team-mates as they have helped me win this award.

The 'Special One' Mourinho missed out on the manager's gong, however, as Garry Monk of Chelsea's upcoming opponents Swansea won the award for Manager of the Month, his team having also secured maximum points from their opening three matches. Mourinho put aside any feeling of personal disappointment to congratulate Costa on his well-deserved recognition:

I prefer my players to be players of the month than me to be manager of the month. I think last season some of them in some moments really deserved it and they never got it. In this first month, if it wasn't Diego or Cesc Fàbregas or Nemanja Matić I would be much more disappointed than last season. Last season it was something I got used to. Finally we have a player of the month, which Diego deserves, but I don't want to focus on Diego. My team deserved that one of the boys be player of the month. The fact the decision of manager of the month went to the Swansea manager is fair.

The ruthless Costa celebrated in typical fashion after shaking off a hamstring injury, helping himself to a hat-trick, the first of his Chelsea career, to inspire his team to a 4–2 victory over the previously unbeaten Welsh side. Skipper Terry put through his own net to give the visitors a one-goal head start before Costa climbed highest to head home an equaliser on the stroke of half-time from a corner. Fàbregas teed Costa up for a simple second shortly after the break before the deadly striker completed his treble from close-range. Replaced with twenty minutes to go, Costa exited the playing turf to a rapturous standing ovation from Chelsea's delighted fans to allow Rémy his debut in blue. And the Frenchman made an instant impact, stroking home from the edge of the area to seal a fourth victory in a row. After Costa's match-winning display, Mourinho attempted to play down the growing expectations on his star forward:

> If the team plays well he has to score goals. Seven goals in four Premier League matches are maybe too much – we cannot expect him to have fourteen goals after eight matches. It surprises me because it's not normal – you cannot repeat it in a cyclical way. He's comfortable in the team. I think now everybody knows Chelsea did the right thing in waiting for him and not going to the market in the last summer of 2013 or in January this year, just to buy a striker. If he keeps scoring a few goals, a few goals gives points and points help the team to be in the top part of the table.

BBC pundit and Newcastle United legend Alan Shearer echoed Mourinho's praise of Costa after watching him destroy Swansea, telling Radio 5 live and *Match of the Day*:

Everything impressed me about Diego Costa today. He is looking the real deal. When it is not going as it should be for Chelsea, they have a goalscorer who can get them out of it. When you consider it took Fernando Torres forty-three games to get seven goals, Costa definitely makes a difference. What Chelsea have now is a guy that, when they are playing poorly, can score goals and pull them through. Chelsea did not play well against Swansea but just before half-time they got a corner and he scored. He is always available. He always wants the ball to feet and if you want to push him around and bully him it is alright because he will do the same to you. As well as goals, he can assist also. He can do pretty much everything. He has made a great start. He will get a bagful of goals this season if he stays fit because that team will create chances for him.

With seven goals in his first four games, the prolific striker gave the thumbs up to his new team-mates for the fantastic start to life he was enjoying at the club, telling the club website:

Every striker has their own way of playing and their strengths and a different team behind them. That is very important. If you do not have the team behind you then you cannot do things on your own. It all depends on the team. I try to play in the best manner, and hopefully things will continue like that. But there will be a moment when I cannot score – that is football.

## DIEGO COSTA: 'THE BEAST'

Domestic competition took a backseat in midweek as Chelsea welcomed Schalke 04 to the Bridge in the opening round of Champions League fixtures. Costa was given a rest by the manager ahead of the weekend's big clash with champions Manchester City, starting the match from the bench and allowing Drogba his first start of his second spell at the club. Fàbregas put the Blues ahead but the Germans earned a valuable point when Klaas-Jan Huntelaar netted Schalke's first goal against Chelsea in five Champions League outings.

With Costa still nursing a slight niggle to his hamstring ahead of the clash between the two title favourites the following weekend, Mourinho gave an update on his striker's fitness:

Everybody is ready to play. Diego is not in the best condition but he will start the game. He plays this game, he won't play against Bolton, and he plays against Aston Villa. Let's see his evolution. The medical department are doing their best, the player is fantastic in trying to play and being available for the team. We have to try to protect him until he gets completely fit.

With the new Spanish international declared fit to start the match, it was title favourites Chelsea who broke the deadlock with seventy minutes played. Costa released the ever-dangerous Hazard down the right and the Belgian's threatening cross was slotted home by Schürrle to the delight of the travelling army of Blues fans. And Costa nearly doubled the advantage later in the match only for the post to deny him a fifth scoring match in a row as Chelsea remained on course for a victory which would prove their credentials as genuine title contenders. Cue all-time Chelsea record goal scorer Frank Lampard to enter the action. Released by the Blues at the start of the season, the Chelsea legend, on loan at City from his new parent club New York City in the MLS, popped up ahead of his old captain Terry to volley home and snatch a point for his new employers, prompting a dismissive Mourinho to tell Sky Sports: 'Frank Lampard is a Man City player. When he decided to go to a direct competitor then love stories are over.'

After their late disappointment at the Etihad Stadium and the end of their 100 per cent record, Chelsea got back to winning ways with a 2–1 win over Bolton Wanderers in the League Cup third round, before welcoming Paul Lambert's high-flying Aston Villa to the King's Road. Chelsea took an early lead through Brazilian midfielder Oscar before Costa, causing the Villa defence numerous problems, rose highest to glance home César Azpilicueta's sumptuous cross to double the advantage, his eighth goal in just six starts. Costa nearly added a third after tormenting Alan Hutton with a jinking run and shot, only for Willian to tap home the rebound to complete a comfortable victory and maintain a three-point lead at the top of the Premier League table over Southampton with six matches played. After the victory, Mourinho revealed the full extent to which Costa's hamstring problems were affecting his ability to train:

He cannot be on top of his game. He's doing almost nothing in training. He's just resting and recovering from the tight muscle he has. I don't care about Diego's goals. For me it's important that the team score enough goals to win. I know a striker scoring goals is always nice for him and for his confidence, especially for a player like him who is not training as he should, because we are protecting him in certain situations.

Brazilian playmaker Willian and ex-Atlético Madrid team-mate and the Chelsea number one Courtois, were quick to sing the praises of their dangerous number 19 after the match: 'He is happy to be here, he is a good player and he is funny, he is joking all the time and I am happy to play with him at Chelsea,' said Willian.

Courtois added: 'Last year he scored lots of goals and this year he has started from where he left off. It's just as important the other attackers score because every goal is worth the same but we hope he can continue scoring like he has been.'

Next up for the squad was a trip to Mourinho's home city Lisbon in Portugal to face Sporting in the Champions League, and addressing fitness concerns over Costa, the Portuguese said: 'Diego starts. Hopefully he plays again on Sunday, against Arsenal, but at the moment I don't think about Arsenal, I think about Sporting and Diego starts tomorrow.'

Costa completed the full ninety minutes against Sporting despite his fitness issues, causing constant mischief to the Lisbon club's defence and seeing a number of chances foiled by the outstanding Rui Patrício in the opposition goal. But it was former Benfica midfielder, Nemanja Matić, to the utter dismay of the Sporting fans, who was to secure a winning end to John Terry's hundredth Champions League match for Chelsea, when his looping first-half header hit the back of the net in a hard-fought 1–0 victory.

Costa collected the PFA Fan Player of the Month award for September, recognising his outstanding start to his time in England, before Vicente del Bosque called the prolific target man up to his Spain squad for the forthcoming Euro 2016 qualifiers against Slovakia and Luxembourg. Mourinho had told the BBC after the victory over Villa days before of his hopes that Costa would be rested by La Roja for the two fixtures:

> If he doesn't go to the national team and if he stays here for fifteen days just on treatment, he has the perfect chance to be top for Chelsea and top for the national team. If he doesn't have this period, it will be always, plays one game, the other is in trouble, the muscle is tight, the muscle is in danger of rupture.

Reacting to Costa's call-up for the qualifiers despite his ongoing fitness problems, a disappointed Mourinho responded in typical fashion, warning Del Bosque that he should not expect Chelsea to send him on international duty in peak condition:

> My reaction to the news that he's in the Spanish squad is to have no reaction because it's something I could already imagine. It's not a surprise for me. Can he play three matches in a week? I think it's too much, but he's going to do that. And why is he going to do that? Because I'm not going to save him to be in perfect condition for the national team. This week we have three very important matches. The Champions League match was crucial for

us after a bad result at home. We needed that victory away so I had to go with everything and everybody. It is an important match against Arsenal, and being the last one in that busy period for the club, he plays. He had the match in Lisbon, he will have had these four days in between, and so he will be in an okay condition. What happens in the days after that [with his national team] is not my responsibility.

Chelsea welcomed major city rivals Arsenal to the Bridge ahead of the international break, prompting a reunion for ex-Gunners captain Cesc Fàbregas and his mentor Arsène Wenger. And ahead of the fixture, asked about the possibility of his unbeaten squad matching the achievement of Arsenal's 'Invincibles' in 2003–4 to go through the whole Premier League calendar unbeaten, Mourinho poured scorn on the idea, saying: 'It's something that happened once in a lifetime. I don't see, in modern football with the competitiveness of this Premier League, one team being champion without a defeat. That will stay in the history as the second and the last time. [That is] my opinion, but we don't know.'

Arsenal posed some early problems for the home team and an ugly first-half challenge from Gary Cahill on Arsenal's new superstar Alexis Sánchez witnessed old adversaries Mourinho and Wenger engaging in a spot of pushing and shoving on the side-lines. However, after a penetrating run from Hazard saw him felled by Laurent Koscielny, the Belgian picked himself up to stroke the resulting penalty home with consummate ease. And a third win in a row at the Bridge over Arsenal was completed when Fàbregas, who had earlier escaped conceding a possible penalty for handball, silenced the taunts of the travelling Gunners supporters with a glorious searching pass to Costa, who after taking the ball down on his chest cleverly clipped the ball over the advancing Wojciech Szczęsny. The victory ensured Chelsea's lead at the top of the table remained five points over second-placed Manchester City and extended Wenger's winless streak against Mourinho to twelve matches.

Costa suffered an unexpected defeat four days later in Žilina as European Championship holders Spain crashed to a 2–1 reverse at the hands of Slovakia. But he did help La Roja to a 4–0 victory over Luxembourg three days later as he notched his first goal for his adopted country in seven games.

Back in the Premier League and with Costa ruled out through injury, Chelsea's fine start to the season continued as they swept East London neighbours Crystal Palace aside at Selhurst Park, Oscar and Cesc Fàbregas' goals guiding them to a 2–1 victory in John Terry's 500th match as captain of his beloved Blues. When quizzed after the match as to the extent of Costa's injury, Mourinho, clearly unamused that his star striker had played 172 of a possible 180 minutes for his national team and picked up a groin injury in the process, retorted to the BBC:

He will be in great condition in mid-November to be back for the national team. That's for sure. He will play for me when he has free time from the national team. After we beat Arsenal, Costa went to the national team, he played two big matches against Slovakia and Luxembourg, and he came back in conditions where he's not available to play for his club. Our medical department will take great care of him and in mid-November he will be in perfect condition.

Costa missed the midweek 6–0 thrashing of Slovenian champions NK Maribor under the lights at the Bridge due to a viral condition that saw him hospitalised, leaving him a major doubt for the weekend visit to Old Trafford and a clash with thirteen-time Premier League champions, Manchester United. Mourinho had been a member of United manager Louis van Gaal's coaching staff during his time at Barcelona after the Dutchman took over the reins at the Catalan giants following Sir Bobby Robson's departure. Drogba, starting in place of the still side-lined Costa, opened the scoring at the 'Theatre of Dreams', his first league goal since returning to the club. However, following Ivanović's sending off late on, Robin van Persie latched onto a rebound from Ángel di Maria's resultant free kick to snatch an undeserved point for the Red Devils.

Two days later football's world governing body FIFA announced the twenty-three contenders for the coveted Ballon d'Or award, currently held by Real Madrid's Portuguese superstar Cristiano Ronaldo. Three Chelsea players made the shortlist, with Eden Hazard, Thibaut Courtois and Diego Costa all nominated for World Player of the Year, and Mourinho one of the contenders for World Coach of the Year.

Drogba's two goals spared Chelsea's blushes in a keenly fought contest with Shrewsbury as the Blues progressed to the fifth round of the League Cup ahead of a weekend derby with West London neighbours QPR. Ahead of the match Mourinho, commenting on Costa's availability for the clash, had another sly dig at Del Bosque saying:

I am always supportive of players playing for countries, when the players are in condition to do it and when the players in the national teams, they follow the same kind of programme to recover from the problems they have. Everyone knows the time Diego was having problems at Chelsea and the way we managed to keep him playing, and then after the national team we lost him for four matches in three different competitions. Now he is available again but he needs obviously to be again under special care and we are going to do that, it is the only thing we can do.

Following a four-match absence, Costa, restored to the starting line-up after recovering from his viral infection and niggling groin and hamstring injuries, combined with Fàbregas to set up a superb opening goal for Oscar. Charlie Austin's equaliser just past the hour threatened to end the Blues' 100 per cent home record before Hazard coolly converted a penalty with fifteen minutes remaining to stretch their lead over surprise contenders Southampton to four points and Manchester City at the top of the table to nine points, although City would reduce that deficit to seven points with victory over United in the Manchester derby the following day. In an interview with the BBC after the final whistle, Mourinho risked the wrath of the home crowd when he criticised the support on offer to his players at Stamford Bridge, saying: 'At this moment it's difficult to play at home because playing here is like playing in an empty stadium. When we scored was when I realised "Whoa, the stadium is full. Good."'

Perhaps luckily for the Blues' supremo, two away games

followed as firstly Maribor shocked the Blues to take a point in their Champions League group game in Slovenia before the guaranteed hostile reception at Anfield as the squad travelled to Merseyside to face Brendan Rodgers' Liverpool. Ahead of the difficult trip to the north-west, Mourinho, in his pre-match press conference gave his reaction to the news that Costa had been omitted from Del Bosque's squad for the upcoming Euro 2016 qualifier with Belarus and the friendly with World champions Germany:

I'm pleased but I want to make it clear I did nothing for that to happen. As you could see he was protected on Wednesday, but because the result was not good I couldn't protect him and I had to play him for forty-five minutes. As a consequence of the work we are doing with him we think he is ready to start the match tomorrow. In the fifteen days after he can rest and work properly. It's fantastic news for us and I obviously thank the Spanish Football Federation for the decision they made, but I want to make it clear I did nothing for that to happen. After the match the plan is for Diego to have a period of complete rest – no training, no treatment – and just let him rest for a few days. After that he will continue the specific work he is doing without having a match to play. It's very good news for him, for us and for the national team, because normally now he has to go in the right direction and it's good for the Spanish Federation to have a good Diego and not a so-so Diego.

## FORWARD THINKING

After crippling Liverpool's charge for the title the previous season, Chelsea got off to the worst possible start when Emre Can's long-range effort deflected in off Cahill to send the Kop into a frenzy of delight. Yet within five minutes the Blues were back level. When Costa found space to nod a corner back across goal, Liverpool keeper Simon Mignolet was only able to parry Terry's header back out to Cahill who forced the ball over the line, confirmed with the help of goal-line technology. The goal at the Kop end evoked memories of Luis García's 'ghost goal' in the Champions League semi-final at Anfield in 2005, but this time it was Chelsea who benefitted thanks to the new technology, which had been sadly non-existent nine years previously.

Costa, who fought a constant running battle with Martin Škrtel, the type of battle he thrives upon, was determined not to let his marker get the better of him as he had done the previous month when the Slovakian defender captained his country to a shock win over Costa's Spain. And after some less than affectionate clashes throughout the game, it was Costa who came out on top when he rammed home his tenth goal of the season to preserve Chelsea's unbeaten start to the season and heap further blue misery on the hosts.

After the match César Azpilicueta praised Costa's infectious never-say-die attitude whilst also praising the strength of the club's forward options:

We are lucky because the three strikers we have are very good. You saw when Diego wasn't playing Loïc and Didier scored goals, and now Diego has come back and scored. He plays with high passion, he's always fighting for the team and, even in training, he wants to score all the time, he's a really good finisher. Even in the last five or ten minutes he was pressing high and doing his job, for the team that's massive.

Following the international break, Chelsea, with Costa refreshed from his time off, welcomed struggling WBA to Stamford Bridge and it was a goal made in Brazil that got Chelsea off to a flying start with just eleven minutes played. A lovely curling cross from Oscar found the Spain striker whose sublime chest control and first-time volley demonstrated again the range of different goals he is capable of producing, his eleventh in just twelve matches. Hazard doubled the advantage on twenty-five minutes before WBA were reduced to ten men five minutes later following Claudio Yacob's ridiculous two-footed lunge on Costa, which earned him a straight and justified red card. The match finished 2–0 despite incessant Chelsea pressure to extend the Blues' lead at the top of the table to seven points and make it a club record ten wins and two draws without defeat at the start of the season.

The squad travelled to Germany midweek looking for the win that would confirm their place in the knockout stages of the Champions League as group winners. And a familiar face would greet them on their arrival in Gelsenkirchen. Roberto di Matteo, the former Blues midfielder and manager of the club when they celebrated the greatest night in their history, winning the Champions League final in Munich back in 2012, was now in charge of the opposition, Schalke.

However, it would not prove a happy reunion with the tteo represented as a player for six years. When

Costa was denied his first Champions League goal within the first minute, John Terry headed Chelsea into the lead from the resulting corner with just eighty-six seconds played, the fastest goal in the competition's history for the club. Willian put the Blues two ahead and from another corner, Schalke defender Jan Kirchhoff headed into his own net as Chelsea took a commanding 3–0 lead into the half-time interval.

Drogba came on to replace Costa after sixty-six minutes and within ten minutes of his arrival put the Blues 4–0 up before he provided the simplest of tasks for Ramires to make it five. A fantastic way to qualify for the knockout stages, but for Costa yet another Champions League match without a goal. For some reason he had no problem putting the ball in the net in the Premier League but when it came to European football it was a different story.

Upon their return from European action, Mourinho's men travelled north to Wearside to face another ex-Blue in the shape of Gus Poyet, head coach for Sunderland. The Black Cats went into the match as the last team to beat Chelsea with a dramatic 2–1 win at Stamford Bridge in April, and Poyet's men once again proved a thorn in the side of Mourinho as they eked out a goalless draw, in the process becoming the first team to stop Chelsea scoring in the league thus far. After the final whistle, Mourinho, despite his team retaining their unbeaten record, claimed that 'only one team were trying to win the game', but the main talking points from the match revolved around the actions of Costa during the ninety minutes.

The Brazilian-born Spaniard appeared to kick out at Black Cats defender John O'Shea in the first half, although the incident went unpunished by referee Kevin Friend. And in the second half, challenging for a high ball with Wes Brown, Costa appeared to catch the former Manchester United defender in the face with a careless swinging arm. On this occasion he saw yellow despite the Sunderland players calling for the card to be red. It would mean a ban for Costa, his first in English football, the yellow card having been his fifth of the season. However, reflecting on the loss of his main goalscorer to the BBC, Mourinho preferred to suggest that Costa's yellow card was the result of 'clever' defending, rather than of the forward's own making: 'Brown is very experienced and he used his body. They can frustrate a striker and can also be clever enough to get cards. But no problem. It's a yellow card. He doesn't play against Tottenham.'

With Costa suspended for the visit of Tottenham in midweek, Mourinho turned to Drogba to lead the Blues attack against a Spurs team looking for their first Premier League win at the Bridge in twenty-three attempts. And before kick-off, Mourinho admitted his confidence that both Drogba and Rémy would prove worthy replacements for Costa: 'It doesn't affect us. We trust Loïc Rémy and Didier Drogba the same way we trust Diego Costa. This is not our way of work, so forget Diego. We trust the other two and we go with one of the other two.'

And the veteran Ivorian forward filled in admirably for his striking counterpart, first supplying Hazard with the opener before putting the Blues two ahead in the first half after latching onto Oscar's through ball. Chelsea wrapped up yet another win at home over Spurs when Rémy entered the fray from the bench to slide home and preserve their six-point lead at the top of the table, with a fourth successive clean sheet.

However, Chelsea's unbeaten run of twenty-three matches for the season would come to a shuddering halt as the team returned to the north-east for the second time in a week to face Alan Pardew's Newcastle United. With Costa restored to the starting line-up after his midweek suspension, Chelsea went in search of Mourinho's first win on Tyneside in five attempts as Blues boss. However, the visitors fell two goals behind when second-half substitute Papiss Cissé's brace of goals fired the Magpies into a commanding lead before Newcastle defender Steven Taylor received his marching orders for a second yellow card. Drogba pulled one back for the visitors when he headed home Fàbregas' free kick and with Chelsea piling on the late pressure, Costa watched in disbelief as debutant replacement goalkeeper Jak Alnwick heroically tipped his goal-bound effort over the crossbar.

Costa once again failed to find the back of the net when Chelsea comfortably beat Sporting 3–1 at the Bridge to deny the Portuguese giants a place in the knockout stages of the Champions League. But the big man was back on target for the Blues in the very next game as the team got back to winning ways in the league to maintain their three-point lead at the top of the table in a fiery win over Hull City in west London. A header from Eden Hazard put the Blues 1–0 ahead after just seven minutes of the contest.

However, controversy was to follow in the second half when referee Chris Foy yellow-carded Costa for a dive even though the forward looked to have been clipped by Jake Livermore on the edge of the Tigers' penalty box. To make matters worse, the league's top goalscorer didn't appeal for a free kick yet Foy still cautioned him, his seventh of the season. Willian had already been punished with a card in the first half for diving and Gary Cahill also received a first-half caution for a bad tackle and could easily have seen red after going down without any apparent cause in the Hull area. But instead it would be Steve Bruce's men who would be reduced to ten, when Tom Huddlestone lunged in on Chelsea left back Filipe Luís to leave Foy with no option. Costa put any personal frustrations aside with just over twenty minutes remaining when he wrapped up the three points with a deft finish from Ivanović's assist.

After the match, Bruce likened the events on the pitch to something out of Swan Lake, while Mourinho, clearly frustrated by the reputation Costa appeared to be earning himself, defended his striker against the accusations of simulation, telling the press:

I can't believe it. I can't believe it. I remember two that are understandable and fair. One was against Newcastle because he complained with the referee with arms in the air in body language that was not accepted normally by the referees and [Martin] Atkinson gave him the yellow card. And the other one in Liverpool, when there was a really aggressive duel with [Martin] Škrtel – you know, fighting in a yellow card way. All the others, the first one at Burnley is a penalty and a red card for the keeper and he gets a yellow card. Other times, it is not a simulation and they give him a yellow card. Other times he touches one guy and it is a yellow card. Everything he does is a yellow card, so he does nothing for a red card; he does nothing, really. For me, the normal situation would be now to be on the second, maximum, third yellow card.

But seven yellow cards – it looks like everybody comes ready for him, which I don't understand. I think when he was [at] Atlético he created a certain image and people don't believe that he can change. People don't believe the way we teach him what England is – the mentality, what people accept, what people don't accept, what is a red card.

People don't understand that he is intelligent enough to understand it and to change – because he changed.

Meanwhile, following the victory, Blues defender Branislav Ivanović preferred to ignore the accusations of diving to reveal his personal opinion on how the Spanish international was settling into Chelsea's squad and style of play:

He knows how to control himself very well. He never sleeps in the game, he's not quiet, he wants to be a star, and he wants to be the player around which everything happens in the game. It's good for the team when he's working and you can see he is always trying to win duels and look positive on the pitch. He is set up like this for the team, it's his style. He's a very nice and funny guy. He likes to make jokes and I think when he improves his English he'll have even more influence in the squad.

Mourinho would afford his main striker a deserved rest against Derby County in midweek as the team earned a place in the semi-finals of the League Cup with a hard-fought 3–1 victory over their plucky Championship hosts. However, unlike in Spain where he had grown accustomed to having the

Christmas period off with the league system shutting down for two weeks, Costa was back in action three days before Christmas Day when Chelsea travelled north to face Stoke City at the Britannia Stadium.

Looking to secure top spot in the Premier League at Christmas, Chelsea got off to the best possible start when Terry headed them into the lead from Fàbregas' corner with less than two minutes on the clock. Costa spurned a glorious chance to put Chelsea into a comfortable first-half lead when he dragged his shot wide after being put in the clear by Fàbregas with only Asmir Begović to beat. And in a match that saw him clash numerous times with Stoke's equally physical central defender Ryan Shawcross and Dutch left back Erik Pieters, it was Chelsea who would grab the all-important second goal when Fàbregas scuffed his shot into the net to ensure top spot over Christmas for the fourth time in the Premier League.

The prospect of winning two consecutive league titles with Atlético and then Chelsea was still a definite possibility. And, with Costa having settled in seamlessly and topping the goal charts, it would be a brave man who would bet against it becoming reality.

# CHAPTER 12

# TITLE CHARGE

'Diego motivates us all. When you play with this guy,
you have to give everything. You can see in every action
and for every ball, he gives his life.'
Eden Hazard talks about Costa's winning mentality
after Chelsea's League Cup victory over Liverpool

After spending his first Christmas in England, Costa celebrated the festivities on Boxing Day in typical fashion with a goal as he helped his team to a derby win over their east London rivals West Ham. Oscar squandered a glorious opportunity to put the team ahead early in the match before John Terry, to the possible wrath of his West Ham-supporting father, touched home Costa's knock-down from a corner to break the deadlock after thirty-one minutes. And with Chelsea piling the pressure on their visitors' goal, it was Costa, who had missed a couple of earlier opportunities to extend the lead, who finished the game off in style. Receiving the ball from Eden Hazard 30 yards from goal, he twisted and turned his markers inside out before dragging his low left-footed shot beyond Adrián's reach and into the bottom corner to seal the points. After watching his team-mate turn on the style with his thirteenth goal of the campaign already, Branislav Ivanović was once again full of praise for his hard-working colleague: 'Diego is a top player and he is producing some magic out there and his goal was a fantastic individual piece of play. We won the ball back and counter-attacked and the rest was down to him.'

The issue of diving came to the fore once again during Chelsea's 1–1 draw away at Southampton. After Hazard had scored his tenth goal of the season with a wonderful individual effort to draw José Mourinho's men level before half-time following Sadio Mané's opener for the hosts, Chelsea once again fell foul of the referee's notebook when Cesc Fàbregas was harshly booked for an alleged dive ten minutes after half-time having being brought down by Southampton's Matt Targett in the opposition area. It looked a clear penalty but referee Anthony Taylor instead opted to caution Chelsea's Spanish schemer to the blatant disgust of Mourinho. Having seen a number of his players, including Costa, unjustly cautioned for perceived diving throughout the season already, Mourinho speaking to BBC Sport highlighted his displeasure with the decision and his frustration with the apparent ongoing campaign against his players:

My view is the view of everybody. There are situations where people can have different opinions but there are others where everybody has the same opinion. It wasn't given because the referee made a mistake, people make mistakes and it was a big mistake. He is a very good ref and a good guy. He is young and has years of football ahead of him, and it is a big mistake, but tomorrow is another day and life goes on. In the first match of the season at Burnley Diego Costa got a yellow card when it should have been a penalty to us and a red card for Burnley, and now a few months later we lose points and Fabregas gets a yellow card. In football we should always try to change the bad things and the double punishment is something unbelievable. You have a penalty and probably you win the game, you don't get the penalty and you get a yellow card.

On the back of the draw at St. Mary's, Chelsea travelled to north London rivals Tottenham on New Year's Day looking to maintain their three-point lead over Manchester City at the top of the table. However, lying in wait for them was a young English striker playing at the top of his game. Costa had put the Blues ahead from a matter of a few yards after eighteen minutes following a swift counter-attack before twenty-one-year-old Tottenham starlet Harry Kane, taking the Premier League by storm, evaded a number of poor challenges to sweep his team level from 20 yards.

Two goals in a minute, the first from Danny Rose followed by an Andros Townsend penalty, following a foul from Gary Cahill on Kane, put Spurs 3–1 up at the break, before the young English striker fired home again from the edge of the area to give the White Hart Lane club a three-goal cushion. Chelsea had conceded four goals in a game for the first time ever under Mourinho. But their hopes of turning the game around gained inspiration when Hazard fired them back within two. However, a Nacer Chadli goal twelve minutes from time rendered John Terry's thirty-seventh Premier League goal, one short of David Unsworth's record, meaningless. The heavy defeat also saw Chelsea surrender outright top spot with Manchester City drawing level with them, on points and goal difference, after beating Sunderland 3–2 at Eastlands.

An under-strength Chelsea got their FA Cup campaign off to a comfortable 3–0 victory over Watford the following weekend as third-round cup fever gripped the country. With Costa sitting out the first half on the bench, the visitors kept the game scoreless going into the break. But following the introduction of Willian and Costa at the interval, Chelsea finally started to play, and goals from substitute Willian, Loïc Rémy and Kurt Zouma wrapped up the expected victory.

Ahead of the home match with Newcastle at the Bridge, Mourinho was hit by an FA charge for his comments after the Southampton match where he suggested there was a campaign against his team. Nevertheless, a goal either side of half-time, the first from Oscar from a quickly taken corner and a clinical finish from Costa in the second half, ensured Chelsea maintained their 100 per cent home record in the league as they opened up a two-point gap over City who could only manage a 1–1 draw with Everton the same day.

Ahead of the match against Swansea at the Liberty Stadium, Costa, the Premier League's top goalscorer with fifteen goals who had also scored a hat-trick the last time the two sides met in September, spoke to the Chelsea website about his time at the club and his hopes for the rest of the campaign:

As a striker, obviously you live and get judged by the goals you score. It is good to get off the mark straight away but more than that it is about the team performance and the hard work. The first goal could have been scored in the second or the third game, or I could have scored in the first and gone through a dry period with no goals, but what is important is the dedication and the hard work and the belief that we can always do better.

If my first goal didn't come in the first few games I would have still been confident. That is because the team we have is such a great one and the ability of the players that play in midfield and feed the striker is very high, so I always knew goals would come. It is just about hard work and togetherness. Fifteen goals is a good mark and I hope to improve it, but more important than my goals is the team is winning. Of course it is nice to be the topscorer but when I came here my aim was to win the league. The most important thing is the club going well, like we did in the other leagues I played in, and it would be nice at the end of the season to see the team doing well as well as the individual.

With Costa once again in fine form against Garry Monk's team from South Wales, Chelsea's 5–0 hammering of their hosts extended their lead at the top of the table to five points. Oscar put the Blues on their way just fifty seconds into the match with a low shot into the corner of the net from a distance, before Costa, on the back of some wonderful build-up play from Fàbregas, Willian and Oscar, coolly slotted home the second with just twenty minutes played. And the prolific marksman made it 3–0 with just thirty-four minutes on the clock when he capitalised on a terrible defensive back pass from Swansea's Federico Fernández to slide the ball under Swansea goalkeeper Łukasz Fabiański. Oscar added a fourth before half-time from a Costa centre and although Monk's team stemmed the tide after the break, André Schürrle, on as a replacement, completed the rout with an easy finish from close-range.

After watching his team-mate, with who he had won La Liga the previous season, take his tally for the season to seventeen, Filipe Luís enthused: 'I've played with Diego for five years now, he's an amazing player and he will get better every year. It's a real honour to play in the same side as him.'

With Costa bang on form and the team five points clear at the summit of the Premier League following City's shock 2–0 reverse at home to Arsenal, the Blues travelled back to Merseyside midweek for the third time already that season to square up to Brendan Rodgers' Liverpool team in the League Cup semi-final first leg, the third meeting between the two for club and country already during the season. And with Chelsea having lost only one of their last seven games against Liverpool before the match at Anfield, Hazard's penalty, a priceless away goal, put them on course to extend that record to one defeat in eight. However, with Costa being kept on a tight leash by Martin Škrtel, and with Liverpool pressing hard for an equaliser, a superb run and finish from England forward Raheem Sterling won the Reds a share of the spoils to leave the tie finely balanced ahead of the return at the Bridge the following week.

Before hostilities could be resumed at Stamford Bridge, however, a fourth round FA Cup tie with Bradford City needed to be negotiated. Bradford, who had become something of a cup giant killer over the past few years looked dead and buried when Chelsea, fielding nine changes to their line-up including a complete rest for Costa, took a two-goal lead before half-time. But a stunning comeback for Bradford was capped in the ninetieth minute when the League One side scored their fourth goal of the afternoon to complete a remarkable fight back and end Chelsea's hopes of an unprecedented quadruple. Openly disgusted by his team's abject performance, Mourinho said after the match: 'It's a disgrace for a big team to lose to a small team from a lower league.'

With Liverpool in town for the League Cup second leg midweek, Mourinho, still smarting from the defeat to Bradford, restored all of his big guns including Costa to the starting eleven as Chelsea aimed to reach the final for the seventh time in their history. And in a thrilling seesaw battle that saw both teams squander excellent chances to take the initiative, it was Branislav Ivanović who would emerge the hero in extra-time when he rose highest and unchallenged to head Chelsea through to another League Cup final, ten years after Mourinho's Chelsea had beaten the same opponents in the final in Cardiff.

Not for the first time, however, the game's main talking points centred on the actions of Chelsea's tigerish forward Costa throughout a highly charged encounter. The Spanish international was in the thick of the action from the start and after appearing to stamp on Emre Can after the two had collided in front of the dugouts, Costa avoided a first red card for Chelsea and a ninth career dismissal after the officials missed the incident. And soon after, the match officials were at the centre of controversy once again when Costa looked to be clearly fouled by Škrtel in the penalty area only for referee Martin Atkinson to bizarrely award Liverpool a goal-kick.

Not one to shy away from a physical battle, Costa found himself at the centre of another furore in the second half when Škrtel claimed to have been stamped on by the Chelsea forward, after sliding in to dispossess the striker in the Liverpool area. The incident appeared innocuous to say the least, much less a stamp than the earlier altercation in front of the dugouts. And in a fiery contest, with the Blues now leading 1–0 courtesy of an Ivanović header, Costa, while battling Steven Gerrard for the ball, ended up scuffling head-to-head with the Liverpool skipper to earn both players a yellow. Costa was afraid of nobody and once again proved he wasn't perturbed by big reputations in taking on Liverpool's iconic captain.

With Chelsea emerging victorious from the tie and a cup final date secured against Tottenham, who would overcome Sheffield United in the other semi-final the following evening, all of the post-match discussion centred around Costa. Liverpool boss Rodgers, having seen his team eliminated from the competition, accused Costa, a player he had tried to sign in the summer of 2013, of foul play after the match in his post-match interview with Sky Sports, who had been covering the match:

These things happen in the game but I think anyone watching it would not like to see what we've seen Diego Costa do. Not just on Martin Škrtel but on Emre Can, a young player who was clearly stamped on. You don't want to see that. There's no need for it. You can easily land somewhere else without having to directly land on an opponent's ankle. It's disappointing to see that on the replay and he was probably very fortunate the referee and the linesman didn't see it.

With Sky Sports pundit and ex-Liverpool captain Jamie Redknapp concurring with Rodgers in his belief that Costa should have been dismissed, Mourinho, wary of getting himself in trouble with FA again, countered:

I prefer not to speak about the penalty. I'll leave it with you because if I speak I will be in trouble and I don't want to be in trouble. What you call a 'stamp' and Sky call a 'crime', I have to say was completely accidental. He [Diego Costa] goes to the ball, chases the ball and the opponent is on the floor. They have contact and he puts his foot there when he's looking to get the ball. These guys [pundits] have a very good seat, very good money, no pressure, they are always right, they never lose, they always win, but they have to be fair and they have to be honest. But, forget it, let's go to Wembley.

After seeing his appeal against a three-match ban for his stamp on Emre Can turned down by the Football Association, Costa was forced to miss the upcoming matches with title rivals Manchester City, Aston Villa and Everton. With Costa suspended, Mourinho called up Rémy to face City at the Bridge and seizing his opportunity, the French international turned home Hazard's centre to put the Blues ahead four minutes before the interval. David Silva pounced on a rare error from Thibaut Courtois to level proceedings on the stroke of half-time, but a disappointing spectacle with Chelsea missing the power and presence of Costa up front, ended with the country's top two settling for a point apiece to see the gap at the top of the table remain at five points.

Chelsea extended their lead at the summit to seven points with a closely contested victory over Paul Lambert's struggling Aston Villa side the following weekend thanks to a stunning winner from Ivanović. The victory saw Chelsea win at Villa Park for the first time under Mourinho's management as Costa sat out the second match of his three-game ban. And following late drama at the Bridge the following weekend, which saw Everton's Gareth Barry dismissed for a second yellow card, Chelsea maintained their seven-point gap at the top thanks to a last-gasp winner from Willian.

Costa was back and raring to go following three weeks kicking his heels on the side-lines when Chelsea travelled to the French capital to face Paris Saint-Germain in the Champions League round-of-sixteen first leg. Recalled to the starting line-up and looking to break his competition scoring duck, Costa told the club website ahead of the match of his hopes to win the competition he came so close to winning the previous season with Atlético Madrid:

I am going to be honest: I want to be a champion with Chelsea, either a Premier League champion or a Champions League winner. I presume that winning the Champions League must be an amazing experience. I reached the final of this beautiful tournament once, but I couldn't win it. We know that our manager is a multiple Champions League winner with loads of experience and that will help. I also hope we are a bit lucky. There are great teams yet to be faced.

Chelsea got off to the best possible start when Ivanović headed home Terry's cross from Cahill's flick to silence the raucous home support in the Parc des Princes. However, having knocked the Parisians out of the competition on away goals the previous season, Mourinho's men were forced onto the back foot as Laurent Blanc's team laid siege to the Chelsea goal throughout the remainder of the match. And with fifty-four minutes played, the pressure told when prolific Uruguayan forward Edinson Cavani headed past Courtois from close-range to level the scores and take the tie back to west London for the second leg in three weeks finely balanced.

The Blues returned to league action three days later with the expectation that they would breeze past struggling Burnley. However, the Clarets, who had given Chelsea a tough test in the season opener, came away from the Bridge with a priceless point in their own battle to avoid relegation. And once again, Chelsea were justifiably upset when Martin Atkinson failed to award Chelsea two penalties, firstly for a handball in the area and then for a foul on Costa. Atkinson, also failed to punish Ashley Barnes for a dreadful tackle on Nemanja Matić, which saw the defensive midfielder issued a red card for his reaction to the potential leg-breaker. To rub salt in the wounds, a late equaliser from Ben Mee cancelled out Ivanović's opener to close the gap back to five points following Manchester City's 5–0 battering of Newcastle.

After the disappointment of dropping points at home to Burnley, Mourinho lifted his team's spirits to secure the first trophy of the season as Chelsea comfortably defeated Tottenham 2–0 at a rain-sodden Wembley, his first trophy since returning to the club from Real Madrid in the summer of 2013. With Matić suspended following his red card the previous weekend, the Blues exacted revenge for their 5–3 New Year's Day mauling at White Hart Lane to send their gleeful supporters back to the west side of London in high spirits as man-of-the-match John Terry and Costa, both with the aid of slight deflections, fired home either side of half-time to give Chelsea their fifth League Cup success and the first silverware of the season.

The team had little opportunity to celebrate, however, with the matches coming thick and fast by now. Three days after their cup final success, Chelsea made the short trip across London to face Sam Allardyce's West Ham United. Looking to maintain their push towards a first Premier League title in five years, a solitary header from Hazard set the Blues on their way and despite facing heavy pressure from the hosts throughout, Mourinho's men held firm to bag a vital three points and maintain their five-point advantage at the top of the table.

While the team remained on course for league glory, Champions League participation ended disappointingly at the last-sixteen stage when Paris Saint-Germain left Stamford Bridge victorious on away goals, despite playing with ten men from the thirtieth minute on. Following Zlatan Ibrahimović's dismissal following a 50-50 tackle with Oscar, Costa, who was enjoying an ongoing physical battle with former Chelsea star David Luiz and Thiago Silva, was denied a clear penalty after his brilliant, mazy run was brought to an end by Cavani's clumsy challenge in the box. He looked rightly perplexed as the referee waved play on. The breakthrough came with just nine minutes remaining when the visitors, despite dominating possession, fell behind to a Cahill shot from inside the box as Stamford Bridge exploded with joy alloyed with relief. Chelsea, a man to the good and a goal up, would surely be in the draw for the quarter-finals later in the week.

However, with four minutes standing between Chelsea and progression, Luiz, returning to the Bridge for the first time since his £50 million departure in the summer of 2013, rose highest from a corner to bullet his header into the roof of the net for a priceless equaliser. 1–1. The match progressed into extra time, and with Costa lucky to still be on the pitch after pushing Marquinhos to the ground after failing to win a free kick for a blatant foul, it was the Blues who struck a seemingly decisive blow when Thiago Silva conceded a penalty for a crazy handball. Hazard tucked away the resulting penalty, but with Chelsea just needing to see time out, Silva made up for his earlier indiscretion to power home a header from a corner with six minutes remaining and send the French champions through to the last eight.

After the match, Mourinho, although magnanimous in elimination, questioned the blatant penalty his team were denied for the foul on Costa, while the forward himself offered his own congratulations to Blanc's team for progressing to the next stage of the competition in an after-match interview with Spanish publication *Marca*:

It could be that the effort during Christmas has taken its toll as we played three games in seven days but it's no excuse. We had enough quality to play a different game [in London] but it was not to be. PSG have a great team and we have to accept it and congratulate them. I hope that next season we will go further than this year.

So for the second season running, Costa would not end the campaign as a champion of Europe, but it says much about the man that he was so generous in defeat and grateful for what he had achieved thus far in his career.

With Chelsea's quest for a historic treble now over, it fell upon Mourinho to motivate his team to set about sealing a Premier League title triumph, beginning with the visit of high-flying Southampton to the Bridge. And within eleven minutes of the kick-off, Costa, with his eighteenth goal of a sensational personal campaign, ended his barren scoring run that stretched back to mid-January when, unmarked, he rose to head home Ivanović's pinpoint centre. Eight minutes later, however, Ronald Koeman's Saints were all square when Serbian winger Dušan Tadić fired home from the spot after Sadio Mané was felled by Matić in the 18-yard box.

But despite peppering visiting goalkeeper Fraser Forster's goal after the break with a barrage of goal bound attempts, Chelsea, with the match ending in a draw, lost the opportunity to stretch their lead over second-placed Manchester City to an intimidating eight points. Yet, still possessing a six-point gap with one match in hand over their northern title rivals, Mourinho's men were looking in good shape to finally bring the Premier League title back to west London.

The following Sunday afternoon, Chelsea travelled north to Yorkshire to face Steve Bruce's relegation candidates

Hull City at the KC Stadium seeking to re-establish their lead at the top of the table after Manchester City's 3–0 victory over West Bromwich Albion the previous day had narrowed the gap to just three. And the team demonstrated its determination to take maximum points back to the capital when just two minutes in, Hazard collected a pass from Costa before rifling home his sixteenth goal of a superb season to put the Blues ahead.

Seven minutes later, Costa doubled Chelsea's advantage when he curled a delightful shot into the top corner of the net to put the visitors apparently in complete charge with eighty minutes still to play. With Chelsea seemingly coasting towards an important three points, two quick-fire replies before the half-hour mark dragged the Tigers level, and with the game entering the finishing straight with the teams still inseparable, things got worse for Mourinho when Costa suffered yet another hamstring injury, forcing the Blues boss to withdraw his main goal threat with fifteen minutes remaining. Any thoughts of settling for a point were quickly dispelled, however, when Rémy, only just on for the injured Costa, scored with his first touch of the ball, his shot sneaking through the legs of Allan McGregor in the Hull goal to restore Chelsea's lead and earn them another priceless victory.

The injury would rule Costa out of Spain's European Championship qualifying victory over the Ukraine. His replacement Álvaro Morata netted in a 1–0 win in Seville, while the recuperating forward would also sit out Spain's 2–0 friendly defeat at the hands of their World Cup conquerors Holland in Amsterdam four days later. However, following a period of rest, Costa was deemed fit enough by Chelsea's medical team to take a place on the substitutes' bench for the clash with Stoke City.

Hazard opened the scoring for the home team from the penalty spot after Fàbregas was upended in the area, but Stoke hit back in the most spectacular fashion just before the half-time break when their Scottish international Charlie Adam picked up the ball deep in his own half and spotting Courtois off his line, proceeded to launch an effort goalwards from fully 65 yards. Despite the Belgian goalkeeper's best efforts to foil the midfielder's outrageous attempt, the ball had too much pace and accuracy on it and nestled in the back of the net for a goal of the season contender to the delight of the travelling Potters' fans and the astonishment of football fans the country over.

Mourinho, searching for some inspiration from the bench, introduced Costa into the fray at the start of the second half as Chelsea went for the win, but within eleven minutes of his entrance, the troublesome hamstring injury that had caused him so much trouble over the past year caused him to pull up once again, resulting in Didier Drogba replacing him. Despite the setback, Rémy, who had started the match as the central striker and had threatened on numerous occasions, capitalised on an error from Asmir Begović in the Stoke goal to once again seal the victory for the hosts who maintained their unbeaten league record at the Bridge.

After the match, Mourinho admitted to BBC Sport that playing Costa had been a calculated risk, one which had ultimately failed but which nevertheless with the team striving for league glory, he felt compelled to take:

If the result was 2–0 he wouldn't play. But I have to risk. My medical department had to risk. If the medical department decide to take four weeks, it wouldn't happen. But no way am I upset with my medical department and I am not unhappy with the will of the player to try and help the team. From all the scans two days ago, the muscle and image was completely clean. The player trained twice at 100 per cent. He did much more in training than he did in the match. The medical department do fantastic things for us. We will wait for Diego again. Next week Loïc [Rémy] or Didier [Drogba] will play.

With Costa once again sidelined by injury, Chelsea made heavy work of their west London derby clash with Queens Park Rangers at Loftus Road, having to rely on a late Fàbregas strike to push their capital neighbours deeper into the mire and towards an immediate return to the Championship. The club cemented their superiority at the top of the pile six days later when Hazard fired home Oscar's pass to give Chelsea a narrow 1–0 win over Louis van Gaal's Manchester United. The victory and a comfortable scoreless draw against Arsenal at the Emirates Stadium maintained Chelsea's ten-point lead at the top of the table as Mourinho's men tightened their grip on the title and extended the Portuguese's run of never having lost a match to a team managed by his old adversary, Arsène Wenger.

After the final whistle, Mourinho responding to the chants from the Gunners' fans throughout the match of 'boring boring Chelsea' in typically belligerent style:

I think boring is ten years without a title – that's boring. If you support a club and you wait, wait, wait for so many years without a Premier League title, then that's boring. This boring team has got the second highest number of goals, has the best goal difference. Only Manchester City have scored more goals than us.

Just two further victories stood between Mourinho's men and the title, and three days after their 'boring' draw with north London rivals Arsenal, and with Costa still on the treatment table, Chelsea recovered from a one-goal half-time deficit against Nigel Pearson's resurgent Leicester City team to seal a 3–1 victory thanks to second-half goals from Drogba, Terry and Ramires. The clinical turnaround was greeted by the expectant Chelsea fans within the King Power Stadium with gleeful chants of 'boring boring Chelsea' in response to the Arsenal fans' taunts the weekend before. It all meant that just one more victory from their remaining four matches would be enough for the club to be crowned champions of England for the fifth time in their history, with Manchester City, their closest challengers languishing thirteen points behind.

The following Sunday would represent the first opportunity as Stamford Bridge, packed to the rafters with the club's expectant fans, welcomed Alan Pardew's impressive Crystal Palace team across London, looking to finish the job and avenge their defeat of the previous season, which had effectively ended their title challenge. And unlike the previous season, when Chelsea who were looking to cement their place in the title race at the time had endured a day of frustration at

# TITLE CHARGE

Selhurst Park with a 1–0 defeat, twelve months on on a sunny afternoon they secured the three points necessary to win the league with three matches to spare. Hazard once again got the vital goal when he reacted quickest after Palace keeper Julián Speroni could only parry his penalty kick straight back to the Belgian, who nodded it gratefully into an empty net.

When referee Lee Mason blew his whistle for the final time it signalled the end of Chelsea's five-year wait for the top prize in English football and Mourinho's third Premier League title triumph in just four full seasons in charge at Stamford Bridge over two spells, vindicating Roman Abramovich's decision to bow to the fans' demands and bring the Portuguese back to the club in the summer of 2013. And for Costa, despite sitting out the previous five games due to his injury struggles, it meant a second successive league title after clinching the La Liga crown with Atlético Madrid the previous season. It was party time at the Bridge as the team, management, owner and fans all celebrated their achievement in succeeding Manchester City as the richly deserved champions.

A week later, Liverpool travelled to west London to face the newly crowned champions and as tradition dictates, the Merseyside club afforded Mourinho's men a guard of honour in recognition of their achievement. The match would also mark the last occasion that Stamford Bridge would host Liverpool captain Steven Gerrard, who had briefly flirted with the idea of signing for Mourinho's Chelsea back in 2005, leading his hometown club against the Blues. Costa, meanwhile, still unavailable through injury, broke with the usual protocol of sitting in the dugout or an executive box as he joined his brother Jair sitting in the East Stand for the match, in the process enhancing his burgeoning reputation amongst the adoring Chelsea fans.

Just five minutes in, Costa, like all the home fans, was out of his seat in celebration when Terry, Chelsea's very own captain fantastic, found space in the area to nod home and put the champions into the lead. However, not to be outdone by his former England team-mate, Gerrard popped up at the back post just before half-time to give the Reds a share of the spoils with neither side able to break the stalemate in the second half.

After sitting out six matches through injury, Costa's name was a welcome addition to the starting XI for the trip to West Bromwich Albion on the penultimate day of the season. However, it was to prove an unhappy return to action for the Spanish international who was substituted by Mourinho on sixty-four minutes, with Tony Pulis' Albion team 3–0 ahead, inflicting only a third Premier League defeat on the Blues in the process.

After spending 274 days – a new record at the summit of the Premier League – Chelsea ran out to face Sunderland on the final day of the season at Stamford Bridge hopeful of ending the campaign in style with another victory before collecting their prize. Costa took a backseat for the match as Mourinho and the Chelsea fans paid a fitting tribute to Didier Drogba, with the Ivorian leading the Chelsea attack from the kick-off as well as taking the captain's armband from regular club skipper John Terry for his last ever match as a Blues player.

The carnival atmosphere inside the Bridge threatened to be reduced to a damp squib when Scotland forward Steven Fletcher headed Sunderland into a shock lead in the twenty-sixth minute. Mourinho was forced to withdraw Drogba shortly after due to injury, to the backdrop of an emotional outpouring of best wishes from the fans and his team-mates. The visitors' lead was to prove short-lived as Drogba's replacement Costa confidently tucked home from the penalty spot in front of the Shed End to drag Chelsea level.

The second half remained goalless up until the seventieth minute when Hazard, Chelsea's PFA, Football Writers' Association and Barclays Premier League Player of the Year, set up Rémy to slide home for 2–1 before the French striker, himself on as a first-half replacement for Juan Cuadrado, added gloss to the scoreline with a neat late finish to prompt the title celebrations into full swing. After the final whistle, John Terry lifted his fourth title as Chelsea captain as the players, fans and management set about jubilantly enjoying their tremendous achievement in winning the championship by an impressive eight points. And following the joyous celebrations at the Bridge less than twenty-four hours earlier, the team and management embarked upon the traditional Champions open-top bus parade around west London as thousands of Chelsea fans lined the streets of the capital to pay homage to their heroes.

For Costa, it had been a wonderful first season in England. A League Cup and Premier League winners medal, a place in the PFA Premier League Team of the Year and twenty league goals in just twenty-six matches was evidence enough of that, on top of which he finished third in the top goalscorer charts behind Sergio Agüero of Manchester City with twenty-six and Harry Kane of Tottenham Hotspur with twenty-one. However, aside from his goals, Costa also endeared himself to the Stamford Bridge faithful and many English football fans in general with his 100 per cent commitment and dedication to the cause, a trait he has always displayed in his career no matter what team he has represented.

In June 2015 a Spanish journalist reported that Costa had been 'offered' to Real Madrid. He was said to be unhappy with life in London. Such reports are two-a-penny in football and whilst nothing can be ruled out, perhaps the best answer to the speculation came from the *Independent* newspaper, with a piece headlined 'Seven reasons why Chelsea have not offered their striker for a transfer.' Amongst those seven reasons given was:

> If you travelled to Stamford Bridge towards the start of last season, you would have noticed a new banner where the Matthew Harding stand meets the East Stand, displaying very clearly 'Diego Costa The Guv'Nor'. Fans quickly took to Costa's all-action and aggressive style and cheered his every touch...

There will undoubtedly be many more prizes and medals to follow for this never-say-die athlete. His effort and commitment will demand it. And then when he finally retires, he will be able to retreat back to his homeland having hopefully done enough to finally receive the credit his efforts throughout his colourful and eventful career so richly deserve.